# IMPASSE AND GRIEVANCE RESOLUTION

## Public Sector Contemporary Issues Series

Edited by Harry Kershen

ᕞ

**Baywood Publishing Company, Inc.**

Farmingdale, New York

This is the first in a series prepared under the direction of Harry Kershen and manuscript editor Claire Meirowitz.

# Preface

This collection of articles on impasse resolution is the first in a planned series of anthologies in public sector negotiations using material first published in the *Journal of Collective Negotiations in the Public Sector.* Future books will include subjects such as collective bargaining in public education, bargaining among municipal and federal employees, and strikes in the public sector.

The articles on impasse resolution were selected for the perspectives they bring to this area. It was the editor's intention to highlight this subject by reprinting studies and expert opinion pieces that would yield information, clear thinking, and fresh viewpoints.

Included in this volume are the solving of collective bargaining impasses during negotiations for a new contract and also the solving of employee grievances during the administration of a working contract. The tools used in solving these problems include mediation, fact finding, and arbitration. The authors of the essays in this volume thoroughly analyze these procedures and often suggest ways of improving the process. In fact, articles are an interesting mix of theory and good, practical advice—from those who have been there.

The articles published here originally evoked great interest, and it is hoped that the present reader—whether teacher, student, or practitioner of bargaining—will find them equally stimulating and thought-provoking, and useful.

Following each article in this book are a number of discussion questions, to be used for stimulating thought and reinforcing concepts.

*Harry Kershen*
Negotiator and Personnel Administrator
Seaford Public School District

# Acknowledgements

The editor wishes to thank those who contributed their time, good will, and expertise in reading preliminary copies of this volume and offering constructive advice and useful suggestions. Their ideas were responsible for improving the flow and continuity of this book.

In particular, I wish to thank Harry A. Becker, Robert Coulson, Kurt H. Decker, Robert E. Doherty, Victor E. Flango, J. H. Foegen, M. J. Fox, Jr., Harold Goodwin, Robert Helsby, E. Edward Herman, James E. Martin, Robert V. Penfield, Harry Randles, Paul Staudohar, William D. Torrence, and Robert E. Wilkinson for their invaluable recommendations.

I also wish to thank Stuart Kershen for his lively and interesting illustrations.

*H.K.*

# Table of Contents

# PART I
# RESOLVING
# BARGAINING IMPASSES

The techniques available for resolving impasses that arise during the negotiating process range from the relatively mild and weak to the strong and powerful. Along this continuum, mediation is the mildest, fact finding a bit stronger, and arbitration—whether called final-offer arbitration or some other term—is the most powerful. Within this procedural thicket, variations can and do occur—supermediation takes place in some jurisdictions, and arbitration may be voluntary or compulsory.

The articles in Part I deal on several levels with these techniques. Becker describes what an impasse is and covers the techniques thoroughly, supplying a good overview to this section and the entire volume. Liebowitz' paper describes the day-to-day work of a mediator: how he operates, on what he bases his recommendations, and so on. The article by Word on fact finding in New Jersey concludes that fact finding is relatively ineffective, leading directly into the following article on strengthening fact finding and the fact finder's role.

Since this part of the book follows the continuum of resolution techniques from weak to strong, the remaining articles in this part involve arbitration. Bellman and Graham suggest consideration of final-offer arbitration, which may be either voluntary or binding, while Fox and McDonald make the case for compulsory arbitration. The following two papers describe how compulsory arbitration has worked in Rhode Island and Michigan. Loewenberg discusses the recurring fear that compulsory arbitration will have a detrimental effect on collective bargaining. His research indicates that such fears are generally unfounded, since compulsory arbitration, properly delimited, has been used successfully in a number of jurisdictions here and in Canada without negative impact on the negotiations process or its end result, the agreement.

# CHAPTER 1

# Public Sector Mediation: Some Observations on Technique

**JONATHAN S. LIEBOWITZ**
*Attorney At Law*
*New York, N.Y.*

Being a labor mediator is a tough job. It is a demanding one in any area of labor relations, and in public employment it is complicated by a host of special circumstances: strikes by public employees are prohibited by law in most states and limited in the others; public employers are financed out of tax revenues and, thus, necessarily concerned with public budget planning and accountability; employer and employee organizations differ in many ways from those in the private sector; the public employment statutes, and the rules made under their authority, are still relatively new and untested.

In New York under the Taylor Law (1967), in Connecticut under Public Acts 811 and 159 (1969, 1965), in New Jersey under

Chapter 303 (Laws of 1968), and in Pennsylvania under the Public Employee Relations Act (1970), experience is just in the process of being accumulated. With this reservation in mind, the purpose of this article is to set forth some observations that are generally applicable to public sector mediation.

To begin with, it is important to bear in mind that a mediator may tie but not bind; he must be a persuader, an arguer to good effect; unlike an arbitrator, he lacks power to require the parties to do or agree to do anything. His power is solely in the confidence he inspires, in the resourcefulness of his approaches, and in his ability to expound them convincingly. This factor more than any other makes mediation such a challenge to the professional in the field.

Success in mediation means settling disputes. Qualifications which aid in reaching this goal include a good working knowledge of labor relations practices, and especially of the making and operation of collective bargaining agreements, and experience in confronting and dealing with different kinds of labor disputes. Add to these ability to work under pressure, to size up conflict situations and to grasp their causes and potential solutions, and sound judgment as to the three W's: *whether* to propose a solution, *what* to propose, and *when* to propose it.

There is no rule book; experts in mediation use widely varying approaches with success. They agree, however, that the negotiators must be led to see that any settlement will be their settlement. They can and should take credit for it—and often use the mediator as a buffer or explanation for having to make concessions—and they must not only accept and live with a settlement, but also take responsibility for "selling" it to their respective constituencies as the best possible settlement under the given circumstances. It is obvious, but often overlooked in the heat of controversy, that the parties will be "living together" long after the particular dispute is resolved.

With this last point in mind, an effective mediator thinks constructively. He can be of great value in hearing out, absorbing, deflecting, and reforming into positive ideas the tensions and even animosities which often arise in labor relations situations. To do this requires an attitude that is hard to achieve: a mediator must be committed and sympathetic to the parties and their interests in the dispute, but he must also have sufficient detachment to avoid becoming enmeshed in the issues and to influence the usually considerable energies of the parties in the direction of settlement.

Fresh approaches and compromise without loss of face must be in the air, and it is up to the mediator to project them and thus to create an atmosphere for settlement.

It follows that a good mediator is a reflective sort. He thinks a great deal, and ahead of the present moment and in alternatives. He anticipates conflicts over issues and how they will surface, and he strives to have several approaches ready to venture at the right time, arranged in his mind according to his judgment of their relative importance and likelihood of being acceptable to the parties.

In familiarizing himself with the impasse at hand, the mediator makes sure he is on working terms with the statute and the rules and decisions under it as they may affect the case. Then too, he knows more than a little about the community in which he is working. He reviews the fiscal and bargaining history. He hears the positions of the parties and their reasons for them; he learns what the issues are and acquires a feeling of how important each is to each side. In doing so, he acquaints himself with the personalities of the negotiators and forms ideas of how to deal with them effectively and in the context of the politics of the situation. Then he builds upon the progress the negotiators have already made (hopefully, there is some) toward his goal: a settlement.

There are many political concerns to be taken into account. A mediator in a public employment dispute deals with people involved in several layers of relationships: that of the negotiators on each team with their colleagues and with those on the other side; then, the relationship of each team of negotiators with the constituency which they represent, such as the members of a Union or of a Board of Education or municipal body; and finally, that of both teams of negotiators to the people of the community at large. In public employment, the bargaining issues are arrayed against and entwined with this ever-present background; a mediator needs a sense of all these relationships in order to be effective.

As the above discussion implies, the writer looks at mediation from an "activist" point of view. That is to say, together with patience, impartiality, knowledgeability, and a reasonably thick skin, the most important quality a mediator should have is an approach. This has nothing to do with preconceptions or rigidity; it entails developing, keeping in mind and projecting to the negotiators an open attitude which leads to settlement of the issues, having a plan for each mediation session and controlling the proceedings, and not being hesitant 1) to start as early as possible clearing the way to reach the basic "gut" issues on which settlement depends, and 2) at the right time, to make proposals to the parties as to how the issues can and should be resolved.

Others will doubtless disagree with this "activist" concept: they hold that a mediator should make it clear that he is ready and able to assist the negotiations in any way he can, but leave it to the parties to go on from there, remaining available but on the sidelines until called upon. The writer's experience indicates, however, that this method is time-consuming (and often there is precious little time to consume in public sector mediation), and ineffectual. The mediator is there because the parties could not resolve the dispute by themselves; everyone is under pressure, and negotiators usually respond well to a mediator with a mission. The more directly the mediator can move the parties toward the goal of settlement, the better for all.

A recent dispute between a school board and a teachers' association provided an opportunity for positive mediation to work. The impasse was mainly over salaries, but there were other issues over which feelings were running high. The parties had been making little if any progress in their joint meetings.

The mediator began by meeting with each side separately to hear its position, keeping the negotiating teams apart from each other. Then, by reviewing the problems with each side and suggesting solutions to them, he succeeded in tentatively eliminating the non-salary issues which had become irritants. Next, he went on to formulate and advance a series of approaches to the impasse over salaries, and by a lengthy process of discussion, evaluation, and reformulation in separate meetings with the negotiators, he aided in bringing forth a solution which each side could accept as fair and reasonable.

This procedure required a great deal of patient listening and considerable legwork. All alternatives were thoroughly aired with each party, and only when each was committed to the terms of a settlement did the mediator bring them together. The final joint meeting was devoted to "wrapping up" the settlement, and because it was conducted at this level, much of the resentment generated over the long course of bargaining was dissipated.

Here then was one approach to a particular situation; each impasse is different, and a mediator must have flexibility and an almost endless variety of resources ready at hand for use as called for.

But in every dispute a focus on defining and redefining priorities, narrowing issues, remaining flexible in negotiations, and not taking positions which may become "frozen" and thus difficult to change—all are essentials which the mediator must encourage.

An important and recurring problem is when to bring the negotiating teams together face-to-face. A joint meeting may be useful at the outset to get things moving, to clear away underbrush issues and to clarify the negotiators' positions on the really tough issues, and useful, too, at the conclusion to iron out final details of settlement and to generate an atmosphere of agreement and continuity.

At other times, the problem is a matter of judgment. For example, where the parties have already met long and often, and advanced and modified their positions considerably before mediation, there may be little advantage in reviewing "laundry lists" of positions on issues. In this kind of situation the negotiators may need to maintain for the benefit of their respective constituencies an image of giving nothing more away. On the other hand, some situations will call for joint meetings well along into mediation, such as to permit parties who have done little real negotiating to learn about and interact with each other across the table. In all cases, the mediator had best be skilled in the timing and use of that invaluable device—*the caucus.*

The qualities of patience and resourcefulness have been mentioned above, and they deserve emphasis. Just when the negotiators become tired and uncreative, and negotiations drag or become abrasive, there is the mediator's cue to come forth with a steady, fresh approach. Neither fatigue nor the rough edges of personality should be permitted to keep the discussions from moving toward resolution of the issues. A mediator should even be prepared to weather some hard going himself to keep things moving. But he can take comfort in the knowledge that with a combination of persistence, sound technical knowledge, and a positive viewpoint, he stands a good chance of success.

## Discussion Questions

1. The author describes a number of attributes a mediator should have. Discuss these and give reasons why they are or are not valuable characteristics in this function.
2. How necessary is it for a mediator to be familiar with statutes, case precedents, and rulings, since he will not be making a binding decision?
3. What are the consequences liable to be if a mediator confronts only the obvious issues on the table?

*Reprinted from Journal of Collective Negotiations in the Public Sector, Winter, 1972*

# CHAPTER 2

# Implications for Fact Finding: The New Jersey Experience

**WILLIAM R. WORD**
*Assistant Professor of Economics*
*Georgia Southern College*

A majority of the states that have implemented public sector bargaining legislation have *not* placed primary reliance on the strike to settle negotiation impasses. Instead, they have adopted procedures that utilize factfinding (and more recently binding arbitration and final offer selection) in an attempt to give public sector collective bargaining a measure of finality. The hope is that factfinding can provide the requisite measure of finality and make a significant contribution to the accomplishment of the twin bargaining objectives of: (1) promoting *bilateral* collective negotiation efforts, and (2) substantially contributing to the conclusion of *bilateral* agreements when an impasse does occur.

To what extent has the initial use of factfinding in the public sector produced these desired results? To help answer this question, a study was made of 63 New Jersey factfinding cases in which reports were written for the fiscal year 1972 (New Jersey's third year of factfinding experience). Information for the study was obtained

from replies of management and union representatives to questionnaires administered during 1973.[1]

## Negotiation Situation Before Factfinding

To gain some insight into the bargaining atmosphere before the
factfinding procedure was implemented, the negotiating parties
were asked three questions. The first question asked whether the
other party bargained in good or bad faith. In 60 per cent of the
cases, union representatives accused management of bad faith
bargaining while management representatives made the same accu-
sation about union negotiators in only 16 per cent of the cases.
Two examples of comments by union representatives to this
question were that public employers should be forced by law to
bargain in spirit as well as name, and that legislation should be
enacted to make awards for bad faith bargaining. An example of
what a factfinder termed as bad faith bargaining occurred in a 1973
New Jersey factfinding case. In this case the city reduced the local
tax rate and then argued for limited raises for police and firemen
based on the criterion of ability to pay.[2]

The second question asked the parties whether their negotiating
positions were affected by the possibility of implementing the
factfinding procedure. The negotiating parties' responses seemed to
indicate that they were influenced to some extent in about 50 per
cent of the cases [44 per cent for management and 58 per cent for
the unions (see Table 1).] In commenting on this question, a union
negotiator suggested that the anticipation of factfinding keeps both
sides from making major concessions and impedes real bargaining.

The third question asked the parties to summarize the actual
progress of their negotiations before the factfinding procedure was
implemented. In over 50 per cent of the cases, the parties indicated
that at best only a small amount of progress (bargaining with a few
concessions) was achieved. A management representative offered
the opinion that factfinding reduces the tolerance level for
collective negotiations and that both labor and management find it

[1] Questionnaires were received for 63 of the 83 factfinding cases during the
fiscal year 1972—a response rate of 76 per cent. The author would like to
thank Jack Chernick, Chairman, Research Section, Institute of Management
and Labor Relations at Rutgers The State University, for his assistance in
supplying the names and addresses for the New Jersey factfinding participants.
Research for this study was made possible by the Faculty Research
Committee at Georgia Southern College.

[2] Bureau of National Affairs, "Government Employee Relations Report,"
No. 530 (September 10, 1973), B-7.

Table 1. Possibility that Implementation of Factfinding Would Influence
the Negotiating Parties' Bargaining Positions

| Reporting Group | Possibility | | | | |
|---|---|---|---|---|---|
| | None % | Slight % | Moderate % | Substantial % | Total % |
| Management | 56 | 29 | 11 | 4 | 100 |
| Union | 42 | 29 | 21 | 8 | 100 |

easier to declare an impasse on the presumption that the parties will go to factfinding and use the factfinder's report as a basis for serious talks.

## Factfinder's Recommendations and Dispute Resolution

One or both of the negotiating parties rejected the factfinder's recommendations in 44 per cent of the cases. [Management representatives had a slightly higher tendency to reject the recommendations (35%) than did union representatives (21%)]. This significant percentage of rejections would seem to support the position taken by a management respondent who suggested that factfinding merely establishes guidelines that both parties may use to come to an agreement.

There were further negotiations in 89 per cent of the rejection cases and the factfinder or another neutral participated in 20 per cent of these sessions. These post-recommendation bargaining sessions together with the cases in which both parties accepted the factfinder's recommendations produced what the negotiating parties indicated were mutual (bilateral) agreements in 61 of the 63 cases studied. For the two cases in which a mutual agreement was not reached, one settlement was imposed by the public employer and the other case was still being negotiated when the questionnaire was returned.

To what can be attributed such a high percentage of mutual agreements after a rejection of the factfinder's recommendations by one or both of the negotiating parties? One positive force appears to be the factfinder. Even though there was a rejection in 80 per cent of the cases, over 80 of the negotiating parties expressed moderate to substantial confidence in their factfinder and in over 60 per cent of the rejection cases a mutual agreement was reached that was a moderate to substantial approximation of the factfinder's recommendations. The position was taken by several management and union representatives that the effectiveness of the factfinding procedure is largely dependent on the strength or weakness of the factfinder.

In addition to the efforts of the factfinder, public opinion and the strike weapon appeared to assist the negotiating parties in reaching mutual agreements. While public opinion was not a significant factor in the majority of cases, it did have a moderate to substantial influence on the negotiating positions of management representatives in over 25 per cent of the cases. (See Table 2.) Strike activity, defined as both actual strikes and explicit strike threats that were acknowledged by management, occurred in one of five rejection cases.

Thus, it seems that the factfinder's recommendations and presence after a rejection, public opinion, and strike activity combine to produce considerable post-recommendation bargaining, which results in a high percentage of mutual agreements. A comment by one of the union respondents, however, appeared to question the *bilateral* nature by which some agreements are concluded. This respondent stated that factfinding is the end of the road; if no agreement is reached, either the employee organization succumbs or goes on strike. One could infer from this statement that without the strike, some public employee unions might agree to the public employer's terms just to get a contract.

Table 2. Influence of Public Opinion on the Negotiating Positions of Management and Union

| Reporting Group | None % | Slight % | Moderate % | Substantial % | Total % |
|---|---|---|---|---|---|
| Influence on Management's Position | | | | | |
| Management's opinion | 67 | 7 | 12 | 14 | 100 |
| Union's opinion | 41 | 24 | 21 | 14 | 100 |
| Influence on Union's Position | | | | | |
| Management's opinion | 67 | 21 | 7 | 5 | 100 |
| Union's opinion | 59 | 24 | 12 | 5 | 100 |

## Analysis

Based on New Jersey's limited public sector bargaining experience, it seems quite possible that factfinding might not actually possess the requisite measure of finality that is necessary to make it an adequate strike substitute. In fact, it is even strike activity itself that apparently makes a contribution to the successful resolution of interest disputes after one or both of the negotiating parties have rejected the factfinder's recommendations.

The need for more finality in an impasse procedure appeared quite apparent from the responses of union representatives to the question, how would you prefer to settle negotiation impasses in the public sector? (See Table 3.) Only 14 per cent of the union representatives mentioned factfinding, preferring instead the strike (40%) and binding arbitration (37%). While 46 per cent of the management respondents mentioned factfinding, a significant percentage (28%) also expressed a preference for binding arbitration.

The problem is that if factfinding lacks sufficient finality now, it might eventually fail to produce the necessary incentive for the negotiating parties to achieve substantial negotiation progress without the necessity of neutral intervention. And, unless negotiation progress can be enhanced, factfinders might be forced into making more procedural (as opposed to substantive) recommendations that the negotiating parties consider as guidelines and thus are frequently subject to rejection. The ultimate result could be the evolution of factfinding into an ineffective bargaining tool.

Table 3. Negotiating Parties' Preferences for Resolving Impasses[a]

| Reporting group | Strike % | Final offer selection % | Binding arbitration % | Fact-finding % | Mediation % | Total % |
|---|---|---|---|---|---|---|
| | | | Method | | | |
| Management | 4 | 4 | 28 | 46 | 18 | 100 |
| Union | 40 | — | 37 | 14 | 9 | 100 |

[a] Several respondents mentioned different combinations of methods (e.g., mediation and binding arbitration, mediation and strike, and fact-finding and strike). The above percentages are based on counting each tool every time it was mentioned.

# Discussion Questions

1.  Why does it seem that fact finding does not possess finality?
2.  How important a bargaining tool is fact finding? Discuss from the point-of-view of both parties separately.
3.  Why would over 40% of union representatives prefer binding arbitration or striking to fact finding?

*Reprinted from Journal of Collective Negotiations in the Public Sector, Fall, 1974*

# CHAPTER 3

# Fact Finding in the Public Sector: A Proposal to Strengthen the Fact Finder's Role

**DR. HAROLD P. SEAMON**
*Executive Director*
*Illinois Association of School Boards*

Collective negotiations in public education provide a mechanism for bilateral decision-making by teacher organizations and boards of education. While most contractual agreements are completed to the satisfaction of the concerned parties, it is inevitable that disagreements will occur in any bilateral endeavor. Determination of the substantive terms and conditions of employment is an area of frequent dispute within the framework of collective negotiations.

Negotiation disputes in the private sector have traditionally been decided by the economic pressures of the marketplace. The strike is the employees' ultimate weapon in the contest of economic power, with the private employer having the countervailing tactic of the lockout. Impasse settlement in the public sector is critical, for unlimited strikes of public employees are illegal in all jurisdictions.[1]

[1] During July, 1970, legislation became effective in Hawaii and Pennsylvania that gives public employees a limited right to strike. Pennsylvania permits strikes only after all impasse resolution procedures, including mediation and fact finding, have been exhausted and provides limitations if the strike endangers health and safety. Hawaii follows similar procedures and additionally requires a 60-day cooling-off period following release of the fact-finding report and recommendations. Also, a 1969 Vermont statute bars the issuance of an injunction in any action connected with negotiations except on the basis of findings of fact by a court after a hearing.

The universal judicial view is that public employees have no inherent right to strike [1]. Compulsory arbitration has been proposed in some quarters, but the many philosophical, legal, and practical problems that must be overcome would seem to preclude any broad-scale movement in that direction.

A wide range of possibilities for third-party intervention lies between the extremes of leaving the parties completely to their own devices as they attempt to resolve their disagreements and imposing a decision for them through arbitration. The terminology describing various types of intervention is not uniform, but two stages can usually be identified [2]. The first stage is typically a form of mediation or conciliation. When mediation fails to resolve the disagreement, a second, more structured, stage of third party intervention may be initiated.

Fact finding is the term often used to describe this second stage of third party intervention. Typically, the parties to the dispute appear before a fact finder or fact-finding panel to present their positions, together with supporting evidence and arguments. Upon completion of the hearings, the fact finder usually issues a public report of his findings and recommendations for settlement. The recommendations are advisory and may be rejected by either or both parties. Fact finding is one phase of an orderly procedure for the resolution of negotiation disputes.

If public policy is to promote a process of free collective bargaining between public employers and employees over the terms and conditions of employment, it is necessary to provide a mechanism that will facilitate the achievement of settlement in the event of impasse. While fact-finding procedures have been introduced in many jurisdictions, there has been little systematic examination of the process. Increased information on fact finding becomes even more important as more and more states and other levels of government adopt the fact finding model in their public employment relations legislation.

The study on which this article is based focused on the process of fact finding [3]. Guidelines are developed for the formal utilization of third parties as fact-finders in the resolution of negotiation impasses. The guidelines are concerned with structural aspects of the fact-finding process and are directed toward improving the effectiveness of fact finding as a mechanism for resolving negotiation disputes.

Fact finding as a procedure for the resolution of impasse has been characterized by "ambiguities in concept and randomness of practice [4]." The recommendations in this article on procedural aspects of fact finding are designed to introduce an element of consistency to practice.

## Reappraisal of the Conceptual Basis of Fact Finding Is Needed

There has been a noticeable lack of clarity and precision in descriptions of the fact-finding process. Methods for resolving impasse can be depicted on a continuum that describes several modes of third-party intervention:

| *Minimal* | | | | | *Complete* |
|---|---|---|---|---|---|
| *3rd Party* | | | | | *3rd Party* |
| *Involvement* | | | | | *Takeover* |
| | | | | | |
| Exhortation | Mediation | Fact Finding | Voluntary | Compulsory | Seizure |
| or | | | Arbitration | Arbitration | |
| Admonition | | | | | |

The presence of the third party becomes increasingly evident and gathers strength and legal force as the continuum proceeds from the point where the third party's role is limited to what can be accomplished through persuasion toward the ultimate extreme of government seizure.

It is difficult to establish the precise placement of fact finding on the continuum, for it falls somewhere in the range between the two most generally used methods for resolving disputes—mediation and arbitration. Practioners have contributed to the lack of clarity in many cases by their utilization of fact finding as a somewhat stronger form of mediation, while in other instances fact finding has resembled formal arbitration proceedings. Certainly there are merits in maintaining a flexible approach, but the absence of a generally accepted conceptualization of fact finding as a mechanism for the second stage of impasse resolution may well have jeopardized its overall effectiveness.

## Fact Finding Should Be a Distinctive Form of
## Third-Party Intervention

It is not inconsistent to urge, on the one hand, development of a unique fact-finding function, and on the other, to accept the proposition that mediation is a preferred technique for impasse resolution. However, combining the functions of mediation and fact finding may well diminish the effectiveness of both. It is sometimes forgotten that fact finding is intended to be a second stage of third-party intervention. Specification of the fact-finding function is essential because it is initiated only after efforts at mediation have failed. The recommended guidelines that follow are intended to contribute to the evolution of a distinctive fact-finding procedure.

## Definitive Fact-Finder Characteristics Cannot Be Provided

There is no persuasive evidence to suggest that a particular set of specific qualifications can effectively be used to select fact finders. In terms of intellectual and personal qualities, it is necessary to reaffirm such generalities as fairness, objectivity, and impartiality.

## "Outsiders" Are Preferred

The fact finder should not be a member of the community within which the district is located, with the obvious exception of large metropolitan areas. An "outsider" is to be preferred because he will more probably be considered impartial and objective by the disputants.

## Knowledge of the Public Education Enterprise Is Essential

The fact finder in teacher organization-school board disputes should have some knowledge of the operation of the public schools, school finance, school law, and professional staff-administrative relationships. This is essential because the scope of issues submitted to fact finding covers virtually every aspect of public school activities. The agency responsible for providing fact finders should conduct a training program designed to familiarize third parties with problems that are characteristic of school district impasse. Such training is important, because the fact-finding hearing is perhaps the least appropriate setting for the fact finder to discover the elements of school finance.

## A Single Neutral Should Serve As Fact Finder

A single neutral should be appointed as fact finder, although a three-member board of neutrals may be utilized in extremely complex disputes. The tripartite board should not be used in fact-finding proceedings.

Individual fact finders are capable of handling the great majority of impasse situations. The single fact finder can more expeditiously schedule hearings and meet time limitations imposed by budget deadlines.

The tripartite fact-finding panel is incompatible with a process built upon impartiality and objectivity, particularly when the process culminates in nonbinding recommendations that rely upon reason and persuasion for acceptance. If recommendations do not receive unanimous approval, they will be largely ineffectual. Some jurisdictions allow each party to select an impartial representative for the fact-finding board. However, the probability remains that the selected fact finders will be viewed as partisans, thereby detracting from the overall objectivity of fact finding.

## Parties Should Participate in Fact-Finder Selection

Procedures for selecting the fact finder should provide for participation by the parties to the dispute. If the parties have some voice in selection, the acceptability of the fact finder, and consequently the acceptability of his recommendations, will be enhanced.

## Mediator Should Not Be Appointed as Fact Finder

It is recommended that the mediator in a particular dispute should not subsequently be appointed as fact finder. Fact finding should be a distinctly separate second stage of third-party intervention. Disputes should proceed to fact finding only after mediation has failed. Presumably the mediator has at some point in the proceedings met privately and confidentially with the parties and has obtained information that would compromise his effectiveness as a fact finder. Benefits are derived from bringing in a new party with a perspective that is not influenced by mediation efforts at prior sessions.

## Issues Submitted to Fact Finding Should Be Limited

Every effort should be made to limit the issues submitted to fact finding. Rigid restrictions should not be set, but some procedural modifications might help insure that the fact finder deals only with those issues that have been major blocks to voluntary settlement. The parties, prior to the initial fact-finding hearing, should be required to frame and delineate the issues that have continued the impasse, indicating in a written brief their positions, i.e., their interpretation of the involved facts. They might further indicate the issues to which they attach the highest priority. In addition, the mediator should indicate his assessment of the issues he believes are the keys to settlement.

## Fact Finders Should Not Attempt Mediation

Fact finders should fulfill a function that can be distinguished from that of the mediator. The fact finder has quasijudicial responsibilities that require him to determine the facts surrounding a dispute, establish the positions of the parties, hear the parties' contentions and interpretations of the facts, and issue a report containing his recommendations for settlement.

Mediation efforts would detract from this second stage of intervention. If the mediator feels that further conciliation efforts could resolve the dispute, then a second mediator should be assigned. Fact finding should be initiated only after all mediation efforts have been reasonably attempted and have failed.

This approach emphatically does not mean that the possibility of voluntary settlement is put aside during fact finding. If the fact finder senses that the parties may be able to resolve particular issues on their own, he should encourage them to resume negotiations and may even recess the hearings for that purpose. However, he should not be a participant in these efforts.

## Fact Finder Should Take an Activist Role in Hearings

The fact finder should take an active part in guiding the fact-finding hearings: questioning the parties, directing further arguments on particular issues if he feels it is warranted, and seeking and corroborating facts on his own initiative. The relative adequacy of the parties' presentations should not be the only factor determining the fact finder's recommendations but, rather, a full disclosure of all relevant information should be sought.

Additionally, the governmental agency administering the impasse resolution process should provide fact finders with as much current information as possible on negotiated settlements and trends in salary levels and conditions of employment. The availability of such an information bank would provide the fact finder with a source of factual data to use both in supporting his recommendations and in verifying the allegations of the parties.

## Attention Should Be Given to the Structure of the Fact-Finding Report

Fact-finding reports should contain five elements that would determine the structure of the report. Reports should contain

1. a brief description of the school district and the sequence of events that led to fact-finder intervention;
2. a clear description of the impasse issues;
3. a presentation of the parties' position on those issues;
4. the fact finder's recommendations; and, most critically,
5. an explanation of the reasoning that led to those recommendations.

## Reasoning in Support of Recommendations Should Be Clearly Indicated

The reasoning that supports the fact finder's recommendations is perhaps the most important component of the total report. The parties and the public might well disagree with the final recommendations but, if the basis on which the recommendations are grounded is clear and rationally derived, it will be difficult to completely disregard the suggested settlement terms. On the contrary, well-reasoned recommendations will be more likely to be accepted or will be used as the basis for further negotiations and settlement.

The reasoning should include, where appropriate, reference to the following categories of rationale. It should be emphasized that the reports cannot neatly refer to considerations in each of the categories on each of the issues. Some categories are not applicable to certain issues, some reasoning overlaps in two or more categories, and a few issues may not be of the significance that justifies extensive reasoning. However, the report may be more persuasive if the fact finder is able to demonstrate that these dimensions of reasoning have been considered.

1. Economic implications must be given primary attention, particularly since economic issues are the ones most frequently at impasse.[2] The fact finder should calculate the exact cost of his recommendations and indicate how the tax rate would be affected. Recommendations should consider the district's ability to pay. This is a difficult concept to implement. The fact finder might well place priorities on his recommendations in districts with a statutory limit on the tax rate. Ability to pay is a more subjective assessment and takes on political dimensions in districts where the board of education must seek voter approval of the budget. Comparative data on all applicable financial factors from surrounding districts will form a more objective basis for consideration of ability to pay.

The other major economic consideration involves the cost-of-living levels that face the district's employees. Recommendations should include reference to documented shifts in living costs and indicate how the settlement would modify the employees' relative position in the economy and the community.

2. Reasoning based on comparative practice, together with economic reasoning, has been given the greatest amount of attention by fact finders.[3] Presentations by the parties have emphasized comparative practice, particularly as teachers strive to maintain parity with their colleagues in other districts. Comparative data, trends, and settlements in other school districts and other areas of public employment should be utilized.

It is emphasized that there must be documentation of comparative data. Criteria that determine the selection of comparative districts should be identified. Reliance on comparative data will be facilitated if the fact finder is supplied with the research support that was previously urged, for this data can be used to supplement the presentations of the parties.

3. The board of education and its professional staff share the common objective of providing the best possible education for the community's children. In the author's opinion, all concerned have given far too little attention to the educational ramifications of their decisions as collective negotiations have evolved. The fact finder

---

[2] Issues classified as economic, those issues whose resolution had a direct effect on the level of funds expended by a district, were found in each of the 70 reports examined. Of the nearly 600 issues at impasse, 56% had direct economic implications.

[3] Each of the 70 fact-finding reports examined included a reference to practices in other districts.

should indicate in his report how the proposed recommendations will affect the learning function and related aspects of the instructional program. Reasoning that considers the implications of recommendations for education should be given increased attention as more and more issues that directly involve educational policy are being negotiated and are subsequently submitted to fact finders for resolution.

4. Although it is difficult to describe with precision, it is suggested that the fact finder give attention to such concepts as fairness and equity in the report as he strives to attain a balance between the competing considerations put forth by the parties. There should be a rational basis for recommendations that affect groups of employees differently.

5. Recommendations are of little value if they cannot be accommodated because of physical or temporal limitations. The fact finder should make an effort to foresee spatial requirements and availability, scheduling difficulties, and practical management problems that might be encountered in administering the recommendations.

6. The use of professional standards, like the documentation of economic statistics and comparative data, can give the fact finder's recommendations increased authority. When impasse issues involve personnel policies, reference might be made to research and standards from the field of personnel administration. Professional guidelines are particularly useful with impasse issues that have a direct relationship to the educational program. Research findings and suggested procedures that are disseminated by state departments of education, other educational agencies, and recognized professional publications might be cited.

7. Applicable judicial decisions and opinions of the state comptroller and attorney general are included in the concept of legal guidance. Fact finders must avoid recommendations of doubtful legality.

It is recognized that an individual fact finder cannot be expected to obtain all this information on his own. The proposal for extensive research and factual support outlined in conjunction with the recommendation for an activist fact-finder role is also applicable here.

It is further recommended that fact finders use these categories of reasoning to guide their direction of the fact-finding hearings. They should indicate to the parties that these are the considerations that will be assessed as recommendations are developed. Such an approach would lead to recommendations that are equitable, legal, educationally sound, and persuasive to persons of reason.

## Distribution of Fact-Finding Report to the Public Should Be Delayed

The fact-finding report should first be issued to the disputing parties. If agreement is not reached before a designated date, the report should then be made available for public distribution. A Twentieth Century Fund Task Force Report [5] summarizes the rationale:

> When it has formulated the terms it will endorse, the panel may decide it will be most effective by not immediately making them public but communicating them privately to the parties. When this technique is followed, a revival of direct negotiations often occurs. The disputants learn the fact-finders' conclusions and have some sense of the public pressure they will be under to accept them when the conclusions of the impartial body that has made a careful study of the issues become widely known.

The recommendations are advisory and the parties in dispute should be given a reasonable period to evaluate the report and carry out any further negotiations that may be needed.

## Fact-Finder Obligations Should End after the Report Is Issued And Questions Are Clarified

The fact finder should be reasonably available to the parties to clarify and resolve any problems of interpretation of the report between the time the report is issued and settlement is reached. However, his responsibilities should end when the report is completed and the parties' questions have been answered. He should specifically not be expected to act as a mediator if negotiations continue. This recommendation is again made to further the objective of developing fact finding as a distinctive second stage of intervention. If the parties do not reach agreement within a stipulated period after the report is issued, a mediator should meet with the parties and, using the recommendations as the basic tool, attempt to aid the parties in reaching agreement. It would be inconsistent with the conception of fact finding proposed in this paper for the fact finder to undertake this task.

## A Final Observation

There is little reason to expect that impasses in collective negotiations will diminish either in intensity or frequency under present conditions, since rising expectations of the teaching profession combine with financial limitations on boards of education and taxpayer resistance to create continuing problems. One development that might ease these conditions is some form of regional bargaining.

There is some evidence that regional bargaining is practiced at the present time. County and state associations make recommendations to their members that result in similarities in the master contracts that are proposed in negotiations. The attention given to comparative practice by the parties when their arguments are presented during fact-finding hearings and the heavy reliance on comparative practice by fact finders in supporting their recommendations indicate that a form of regional bargaining is even now being practiced.

Discussion of the implications of large-scale collective negotiations is beyond the scope of this article. For example, patterns of financing education must be revised. A bargaining structure will have to be designed that permits necessary variations in local districts. Whatever bargaining model emerges, it does appear that there will continue to be an important role for the third party.

The early use of neutrals in the negotiations process might help to diminish the frequency of crisis situations that characterize collective bargaining. Neutral third parties in this context attempt to create an atmosphere of problem solving as they provide objective reactions to proposals, assist in new ways of approaching problems, provide suggestions for alternative choices, and introduce a long term perspective and elements of the public interest [6].

While it is hoped that the frequency of negotiation disputes will be reduced by more imaginative use of neutrals, it is inevitable that some deadlocks will continue to occur. The fact-finding process proposed in this article would be particularly effective in these circumstances.

Regional negotiations would diminish the number of mediators and fact finders needed for intervention. Rather than relying on part-time personnel who serve on an *ad hoc* basis, it would be possible to develop a highly-qualified, well-trained, select corps of mediators and fact finders who would devote their full efforts to collective negotiations. These fact finders would be supported by extensive research efforts and data collection systems that would aid in eliminating many of the factual inconsistencies that are found in presentations during fact finding.

A process that is truly a second stage of third-party intervention would evolve if a diminished incidence of fact finding were combined with fact finders who follow the procedural guidelines recommended in this study. The randomness of practice that characterizes much of fact finding today would be eliminated. Fact finding might then become a mechanism that would be more effective in bringing stability to employer-employee relationships.

## REFERENCES

1. E. Edmund Reutter, Jr. and Robert R. Hamilton, *The Law of Public Education*, p. 412, Foundation Press, Inc., Mineola, N.Y., 1970.
2. Robert H. Chanin, *Negotiation in Public Education: Developing a Legislative Framework*, p. 21, Education Commission of the States, Denver, 1969.
3. Harold P. Seamon, Jr., *Fact Finding in the Resolution of Teacher Organization-School Board Impasse During Collective Negotiations, with Particular Reference to New York State*, Unpublished Ed.D. dissertation, Teachers College, Columbia University, 1971. The study developed guidelines for the formal utilization of third parties as fact finders in teacher organization-school board negotiation disputes. Structural issues in three areas formed a framework for the study: a) qualifications, selection, and assignment of fact finders; b) the fact-finding hearing; and c) the fact-finding report and recommendations. Literature was reviewed to synthesize varying viewpoints on structural issues. One report from each of 70 fact finders who filed reports during a one-year negotiations period was analyzed with particular attention being given to the rationale supporting fact-finder recommendations.
4. Jean T. McKelvey, "Fact Finding in Public Employment Disputes: Promise or Illusion?" *Industrial and Labor Relations Review*, XXII: 528, July, 1969.
5. *Pickets at City Hall: Report and Recommendations of the Twentieth Century Fund Task Force on Labor Disputes in Public Employment*, p. 24, Twentieth Century Fund, New York, 1970.
6. For an example of such a proposal, see Neil Chamberlain, "Neutral Consultants in Collective Bargaining," *in* National Academy of Arbitrators, *Proceedings of Fifteenth Annual Meeting*, Pittsburgh, Pa., 1962.

## Discussion Questions

1. Discuss whether strengthening the fact finder's role is possible, necessary, and useful.
2. Discuss the author's recommendation that the fact finder come from outside the community facing the dispute. What are the pros and cons of this?
3. Do you believe that if the parties participate in selection of a fact finder, they will be more likely to accept his recommendation? Why? Why not?

*Reprinted from Journal of Collective Negotations in the Public Sector, Spring, 1974*

# CHAPTER 4

# A Suggested Remedy for Refusal to Bargain in the Public Sector: Final Offer Arbitration

**HOWARD BELLMAN**
*Commissioner*
*Wisconsin Employment Relations Commission*

**HARRY GRAHAM**
*Lecturer, School for Workers*
*Associate Director*
*Industrial Relations Research Institute*
*University of Wisconsin, Madison*

When a major strike threatens to disrupt an important service, a sense of hopelessness often pervades the public. Publicity about the impasse sometimes tends also to make our entire system of industrial relations appear chaotic. The public wants to know, why can't these disputes be prevented? If the parties themselves cannot agree, why shouldn't they be told what to do? Why can't we have a law that prevents these disruptions [1].

In the area of government employment it has become common for public servants to strike, notwithstanding legislated prohibitions or the strictures of common law. Even members of protective services, the police, and firefighters, have resorted to explicit strike action or

The views expressed in this article do not necessarily reflect the views of the Wisconsin Employment Relations Commission.

quasi strikes. Faced with disruption of garbage pick-up, the education of their children, the protection of their homes and persons, the public has often responded with the traditional American complaint, "there oughta be a law." In fact, a majority of the states have responded to the demand for a law with legislation that prohibits strikes by public employees and some have made attempts to substitute for the strike other impasse resolution devices such as mediation and factfinding. The search for the holy grail of justice and equity to all parties continues as legislatures look for a mechanism for satisfying employees and other citizens, without disruption of important public services.

As of the Fall of 1973, 17 states have enacted legislation providing some form of arbitration for impasses in the public sector. While historically both union and management spokesmen have been united in their opposition to arbitration of new contract terms, that opposition may be less vigorous than in prior years. No less an authority than George Meany [2], President of the AFL-CIO, has commented that binding arbitration should be considered as one way of resolving impasses. Reporting to the National Academy of Arbitrators, Professor Jack Steiber [3] of Michigan State University noted that the results of a survey he had conducted among employer and union officials gave reason to believe that management and labor "may be more amenable to voluntary arbitration of contract disputes than has been generally assumed." Union leaders who have opposed compulsory arbitration of new contract terms in the past now seem to be more disposed to consider it. For instance, Jerry Wurf [4], President of the State, County and Municipal Employees, has noted, "the public is inclined toward compulsory arbitration . . . it appears an easy way of eliminating strikes. As long as we cannot agree on an appropriate impasse procedure the public may be totally justified in demanding a third party neutral . . . We have been impressed by the awards for employees (from compulsory arbitration) . . . and may someday horrify you by lobbying for compulsory arbitration." While that day has not yet arrived, Wurf's comments may be a straw in the wind. Certainly the acceptance, in 1973, by the Steelworkers Union of arbitration of unresolved new contract issues, although in the private sector, may indicate that union opposition to the idea is not as strong as in the past.

Though union attitudes may be changing, unions have by no means embraced arbitration. Ross Atwood [5], Research Director of the Firefighters has accused management around the nation of forcing unions into arbitration of new contract terms at great expense to the union and then refusing to implement the terms of arbitration awards, thus forcing unions into court with its attendant costs and delays. David Selden [6], President of the American Federation of Teachers, has also reiterated his union's opposition to arbitration of new contract terms.

Management officials, too, seem to be changing their long-standing opposition to arbitration of new agreements. Mayor Kenneth Gibson [7] of Newark, New Jersey has stated that "compulsory and binding arbitration of bargaining impasses is an acceptable alternative to granting public employees the right to strike." Former Governor Nelson Rockefeller [8] of New York State, commenting on the Taylor Law, noted that when all procedural steps have been exhausted, "voluntary arbitration makes sense."

The opinion of "experts" in industrial relations is currently mixed, with some leading neutrals willing to consider arbitration of new contract terms. Robert Howlett [9], Chairman of the Michigan Employment Relations Commission feels that examination of the effects of binding arbitration has "showed it will work successfully." On the other hand, Theodore Kheel, the prominent mediator and arbitrator [10], has often reiterated his feeling that any "overall system of compulsory arbitration must ultimately break down," and Robert Coulson [11], President of the American Arbitration Association, is of the opinion that "impasse arbitration should not be encouraged as an easy substitute for the responsibility of public and union officials to reach agreement on the basis of bargaining power ... it encourages negotiators to avoid responsibility ..."

Despite the lack of unanimity by labor, management, and expert opinion, the states have proceeded to enact legislation that prohibits the strike and substitutes some method of dispute settlement for trial by economic strength. In Wisconsin, for example, the Municipal Employment Relations Act governs collective bargaining at the county and municipal level [12]. The statute prohibits strikes and sets forth a series of unfair labor practices, including the prohibited practice of refusing to bargain collectively. While this provision is in the Wisconsin statute, enforcement is often frustrating to the complainant because the remedies do not reach the underlying problems, which may include a philosophical rejection of collective bargaining as a means of setting the terms of employment and/or a basic imbalance of economic power on one side or the other [13]. In view of the more open mind prevailing today on the issue of interest arbitration and perhaps a greater disposition to experiment with it than in the past, the following proposal is offered as the basis for discussion and consideration.

It is proposed that the agency which enforces the duty to bargain be authorized by specific statutory and, if necessary, constitutional provisions, to include among the remedies available to it in appropriate cases, last-offer final and binding interest arbitration of the matter in dispute. Thus, in cases of relatively blatant severe refusals to bargain, the agency might, in its discretion, order the parties to submit the proposals on the table at the time of the violation to such arbitration. The arbitrator would promptly select such proposals as he finds most acceptable in accordance with the statutory scheme and criteria, and impose such proposals as the parties' "settlement." By this means the parties surely would have their legal contentions ruled upon, possibly have their negotiations settled, and where appropriate the aggrieved would have a real remedy. Some strikes would be avoided as the situation became defused.

Whereas in the private sector unions may employ the unfair labor practice strike as a counter to an employer's refusal to bargain[1] and such strikes may serve to resolve negotiations deadlocks, the proposed procedure would provide an impasse settlement method for the public sector without disruption of services and one that is equally accessible to employers. The authors are impressed that public sector impasses may be more troublesome than their private sector counterparts, even when there is no disruption, because of statutory budget deadlines and other peculiarities of government.

Moreover, this remedy would offer a strong stimulus for "reasonable" position-taking throughout the negotiations. The parties would be aware that should they commit *or complain of* a substantial violation of the bargaining obligation, and should such a suit succeed, they would, in a sense, be stuck with their own bargaining positions. Therefore, a major benefit of the scheme should be the generation of a constant pressure from the beginning of negotiations compelling moderate proposals.

On the other hand, one of the most negative aspects of compulsory interest arbitration, i.e., that it extracts the urgency from the negotiations that precede it, is avoided. Under the proposed procedure, the speculation that must occur regarding problems of proof and the ever-static duty to bargain will tend to moderate the positions of all the parties who cannot be absolutely sure as to their

---

[1] It seems likely that the greatest number of unfair labor practice strikes are founded on bargaining duty violations, rather than acts of interference, discrimination, etc. On this basis the proposed procedure may operate, not only as a strike substitute, but as a means of placating employees whose employers have been provocative and have "unclean hands."

compliance with the duty, or of their ability to sustain a complaint of a violation. Only the party who is certain that it can prove that its adversary is in violation of the duty to bargain, and that its own bargaining proposals are more acceptable, may proceed confidently.

It is not the authors' intent to engage in the debate over legalizing strikes. The proposal made herein can be part of a statutory scheme that legalizes all, some, or no strikes. Similarly, it may operate in a system that also provides for fact finding or interest arbitration of some or all impasses on other grounds. It could be available to struck employers if strikes were declared to be a violation of the duty to bargain, or strikes that followed such arbitrations could be subject to greater penalties than other strikes. (Indeed, the proposed remedy might also be appropriate as part of a private sector scheme that limits the right to strike or seeks to inhibit striking because of the critical nature of the product or service provided.)

Last-offer arbitration is suggested because it provides the secondary effect of moderating proposals, which would not flow from arbitration that allowed for the design by the arbitrator of the "agreement" to be reached. There are variations of last-offer arbitration including the form that requires a choice of one party's entire "package," that which allows the arbitrator to construct a "package" by choosing among the parties' proposals on each subject in contention, and combinations of these. The instant proposal does not require a choice among these variations.

It is recognized that there is a potential in this procedure for delay while the alleged bad-faith bargaining is litigated. However, this potential presently exists and is not infrequently realized, but without any resolution of the underlying dispute. Of course, the magnitude of such delays is to a great extent the responsibility of the administering agency and can therefore be minimized by adjustments at that point.[2]

It is contemplated that the administering agency would have discretion to determine that some cases are not sufficiently serious to require this remedy. (Of course, this remedy would not be appropriate to refusal-to-bargain cases except those of the conduct-of-negotiations variety. Cases of violative unilateral action and refusals to provide information, for example, would not call for this remedy.)

---

[2] "Freezing" the parties' bargaining position at the point of violative conduct for the purposes of this procedure should not, and need not, preclude compromise thereafter. But it is essential that the process be speedy and that the time that elapses during its pendency not be excessive. Where at least one party is not confident of its case for arbitration, such a factor may promote some further negotiations.

This procedure might also require some bargaining technique adjustments by the parties. They would need such evidence as could prove their bargaining position at the time of the violation. Presumably, good notetaking would be invaluable. But, this procedure should not rigidify the parties' positions in that presumably the more compromise they evidence, the more likely it becomes that their position will prevail in arbitration.

The truism that the legal duty to bargain has only a minor effect upon the parties' respective bargaining table accomplishments, which are in fact determined more by economic or political strength, is slightly eroded by this procedure. It would tend to improve the prospects of otherwise dominated parties, whether they are unions or employers. In this respect, the procedure is another way toward moderation.

## REFERENCES

1. Theodore W. Kheel, "Is the Strike Outmoded?" U.S. Department of Labor, *Monthly Labor Review*, p. 35, Sept. 1973.
2. George Meany, "Interview with AFL-CIO President Meany," Bureau of National Affairs, Inc., *Labor Relations Yearbook-1970*, p. 276.
3. Jack Steiber, "National Academy of Arbitrators' Meeting," Bureau of National Affairs, Inc., *Labor Relations Yearbook-1970*, p. 150.
4. Jerry Wurf, "Government Sponsors Public Sector Labor Conference," Bureau of National Affairs, Inc., *Government Employee Relations Report*, Report No. 429, pp. B-14, B-15, Nov. 29, 1971.
5. Ross Atwood, "Florida Public Employees View Prospects for Bargaining Law," Bureau of National Affairs, Inc., *Government Employee Relations Report*, Report No. 488, p. B-11 January 29, 1973.
6. David Selden, "Kheel and Union Leaders Object to Curbs on Public Worker Strikes," Bureau of National Affairs, Inc., *Government Employee Relations Report*, Report No. 444, p. B-14, March 20, 1972.
7. Kenneth Gibson, "Newark Mayor Urges Binding Resolution of Impasses in Public Sector Bargaining," Bureau of National Affairs, Inc., *Government Employee Relations Report*, Report No. 453, p. B-11, May 22, 1972.
8. Nelson Rockefeller, "Voluntary Arbitration Under Taylor Law Seen as Road to Economic Peace," Bureau of National Affairs, *Government Employee Relations Report*, Report No. 502, p. B-17, May 7, 1973.
9. Robert G. Howlett, "Ohio Conference on Labor Relations Law," Bureau of National Affairs, Inc., *Labor Relations Yearbook-1972*, p. 117.
10. Theodore W. Kheel, "Kheel and Union Leaders Object to Curbs in Public Worker Strikes," Bureau of National Affairs, Inc., *Government Employee Relations Report*, Report No. 444, p. B-14, March 20, 1972.

11. Robert Coulson, "AAA President Cautions Against Increased Use of Legislated Public Sector Compulsory Arbitration," Bureau of National Affairs, Inc., *Government Employee Relations Report*, Report No. 475, p. B-7, October 23, 1972.
12. *Wisconsin Statutes*, Chapter II, Subchapter IV, Sec. 111:70.
13. The duty to bargain generally does not require any concessions, and labor relations agencies are generally precluded from requiring agreement to any proposals. On this basis the usual remedy ordered in the cases pertinent hereto is an order to return to negotiations with a good-faith attitude. See John H. Fanning, "Remedies for Unfair Labor Practices," Industrial Relations Research Association, *Proceedings of the Twenty-Third Annual Winter Meeting*, pp. 244-253, Detroit, 1970, and *H. K. Porter Co.*, NLRB 397 U.S. 99, 1970.

\*                    \*                    \*

Howard Bellman has served with the Wisconsin Employment Relations Commission for many years and was appointed Commissioner in 1973. He is also a member of the National Academy of Arbitrators.

Harry Graham is the Associate Director of the Industrial Relations Research Institute at the University of Wisconsin. He is also on the faculty of the School for Workers.

## Discussion Questions

1. Compare and contrast final-offer arbitration to other forms of arbitration.
2. Discuss the merits of voluntary and compulsory arbitration.
3. In what ways would final-offer arbitration change the parties' operating procedures at the bargaining table and during bargaining preparations? Why?

Reprinted from *Journal of Collective Negotiations in the Public Sector, Spring, 1974*

# CHAPTER 5

# The Need for Compulsory Arbitration

**DR. M. J. FOX, JR., P.E.**
*Associate Professor*
*of Industrial Engineering*
*Texas A&M University*

**DR. L. B. MC DONALD**
*Human Factors Specialist*
*Midwest Research Institute*
*Kansas City, Mo.*

To many people collective bargaining is the cornerstone of the American economic system. There is no doubt that collective bargaining is the best means of resolving interest disputes between employer and employee. Unfortunately many of the bargaining sessions reach an impasse even though both parties are bargaining in good faith. This impasse generally leads to a strike because without the strike's economic pressure neither side has any incentive to compromise. This contest of economic power would be fine if only the combatants were involved. However, the public often suffers because its supply of the organization's products or services is curtailed. In certain key organizations this curtailment of production or services cannot be tolerated due to the impact on society as a whole. If impasses occur and strikes are intolerable, then some way must be found to resolve the disputes. One proposed method is voluntary arbitration. If the combatants cannot agree to arbitrate, then the next step is compulsory arbitration. There are different types of compulsory arbitration, and each has its pros and cons. The premise of this paper is that compulsory arbitration is necessary in some areas and desirable in others.

The ideal method for settling disagreements is for the two parties to negotiate a settlement. In the give-and-take of collective bargaining, the two sides can trade off concessions in an effort to reach a compromise acceptable to both parties. Cullen [1] stated that " . . . the case for free collective bargaining is unassailable . . . In the abstract, no one is ever against liberty or for compulsion." In discussing possible antistrike legislation, Senator Wayne Morse [2] stated, "It is a situation that attacks, in my judgement, some basic foundations of economic freedom in this Republic." Senator Barry Goldwater [2] stated that " . . . if this is forced upon the American people, it can mean price control, wage control, quality control, and even place of employment control." But for collective bargaining to be effective, there must always be the threat of a strike. This weapon has been useful in the past, but in the highly interdependent society of today it could be losing its effectiveness. George Meany [3] asserted, "We are getting to the point where a strike doesn't make sense in many situations." He went on to state that employers and unions are now so strong that confrontations become Gargantuan struggles that hurt everybody. The Brotherhood of Railroad Trainmen [4] believes that the effectiveness of the strike is being lessened. Automation is curbing the ability of a strike to inflict economic losses on management. For these reasons it is believed that strikes will be utilized less often in the future than in the present.

The prevalent economic theory of today asserts that industry is created by our society and will be allowed to survive only as long as it contributes to the well-being of society. Therefore, when there is a threat to cut off society's supply of goods and services, the public welfare should receive first consideration. Cullen [1] argued that "in cases of doubt concerning the ultimate length and impact of a major strike, the doubt should be resolved in favor of protecting society as a whole." The general public seemed to agree with this argument, as shown by a Gallup poll after the 1959 steel strike which indicated that 59% of those surveyed were in favor of compulsory arbitration of all labor disputes that might result in nationwide strikes. Critics of strike controls point to the fact that a very small percentage of labor-management negotiations lead to strikes. Raskin [5] pointed out that in 1961 and 1962 less time was lost on strike than on coffee breaks. The fact that the great majority of negotiations are settled without strikes ignores the fact that among the major industries, national strikes occur all too often. Therefore, when the discussion is limited to the more critical industries of our nation, the low percentage argument loses much of its weight. Critics of strike controls also argue that the effects of national strikes on the public welfare are grossly exaggerated [1]. They further argue that governmental interference in collective bargaining will lead to a serious weakening of the process. Cullen [1] rebutted these assertions by pointing out that "the government has in fact intervened in most major strikes, thereby undermining the argument that we have seldom suffered emergencies from strikes in the past and also demonstrating that intervention is not a fatal blight upon collective bargaining." The arguments against strike controls were generally formulated during a period when management held the balance of power and society was much more loosely intertwined. In our present society the labor unions in the major industries are at least as powerful as management. Our society has become so interdependent that a bottleneck at one point may wreak havoc throughout the system. Raskin [5] pointed out that "what has changed the arena of industrial conflict—and what demands a change in the ground rules governing that conflict—is the extent to which the community has become the victim in the crisis strikes. The squeeze is much less acute on the economic warriors than it is on the public."

When considering the public interest, it becomes difficult to distinguish between public services and critical industries. While the major industries are probably not as critical on a short-term basis as police and fire protection, they are probably as critical on a long-term basis as sanitation services. Therefore, many of the arguments for compulsory arbitration in the public sector apply equally well to the critical industries in the private sector.

There are many specific arguments for and against compulsory arbitration. Schwartz [6] lists four reasons why compulsory arbitration should not be instituted. His first reason was that compulsory arbitration is inconsistent with the democratic form of government. Seinsheimer [3] disagreed and asked:

> . . . is it democratic to permit a few public employees to subject the *many* citizens of a community or the nation to the perils and chaos of a strike of police or firemen, or the health hazards of a strike of sanitation department employees? . . . In my opinion, the answer to this should be no *if* the arbitration process is mandatory on both parties to an interest dispute.

Schwartz's second reason was that compusory arbitration will minimize and eliminate free collective bargaining. Stevens [7] disagreed and commented that " . . . it seems quite possible that a threat to arbitrate, much like a threat to strike, might invoke the negotiatory processes of concession and compromise which are characteristic of normal collective bargaining." In addition, Stevens proposed an improvement in the compulsory arbitration process to stimulate bargaining between parties. This improvement is discussed later in this paper. Schwartz's third reason was that you cannot force workers to remain on an intolerable job. Seinsheimer [3] agreed and pointed out that laws prohibiting strikes have been almost impossible to enforce because authorities cannot jail several thousand people at a time. This argument against compulsory arbitration actually applies to all forms of strike prohibitions. But if the reader accepts the argument that certain strikes must be prohibited in the public interest, then compulsory arbitration is likely to be as effective as any other measure. It is the authors' opinion that, while compulsory arbitration will not bring an end to all strikes, it will lead to fewer strikes than we are presently experiencing. Schwartz's fourth argument was that awards would be affected by prevailing political moods. This argument was supported by the Brotherhood of Railroad Trainmen [4] who added that public relations campaigns and lobbying would also be a factor. However, these arguments apply equally well to the current strike controls. It is felt that compulsory arbitration would lead to greater equity than the current controls. This is because the compulsory arbitration system would be bound by rules and procedures, administered by professionals instead of politicians, and subject to appeal to the courts.

Schwartz was not the only writer to present arguments against compulsory arbitration. Denise [8] asserted that both parties in negotiations will hold back their final offer to give the arbitrator room to maneuver. This problem was also addressed by Stevens and will be discussed later. Cullen [1] discussed three methods by which labor and management can settle negotiations without strikes—voluntary arbitration, partial operation, and non-stoppage strike. Since none of the methods is presently experiencing widespread use, we must assume that labor and management will not institute them until given an incentive to do so. It is felt that the introduction of compulsory arbitration as a last step in negotiations might provide just such an incentive. Many strike control critics say that the public is adequately protected from strikes by the present laws. The Brotherhood of Railroad Trainmen [4] stated that "the present system of governmental intervention provides no guarantee for the public welfare in the case of a national emergency strike." Another criticism of compulsory arbitration is that the negotiators may use arbitration as a face-saving device. Lowenberg [9] supported this contention with case histories. No rebuttal is available for this argument and admittedly the case load of arbitrators may be increased because of this problem. Another argument against compulsory arbitration, contended the Brotherhood of Railroad Trainmen [4] is that "the arbitrator may or may not have the expert knowledge necessary to render an effective and equitable award." On this issue Cullen [1] commented that "to the charge that arbitrators have no firm guidelines by which to decide contract issues 'correctly,' the response is that this is true but neither have the parties, and an experienced neutral can usually spot several clues to a 'reasonable' settlement (such as the terms of other current settlements)." The above arguments clearly show that the experts are divided on the subject of compulsory arbitration, and none of them have an answer immune from attack.

Some of the more eloquent statements in favor of compulsory arbitration are quoted below. In the wake of the West Coast Longshoremen's strike, Raskin [5] stated:

> The unblinkable lesson . . . is that the absence of an explicit legal foundation for government action to defend the public engenders a bargain-basement scramble for solutions that rarely solve anything. The frequency with which our national, state, and municipal officials are turned down or ignored when they plead for reasonableness and restraint to advance the common good is not only demeaning for them but destructive of respect for democratic government. Too often the upshot is capitulation to the stronger and more obstructive of feuding parties, with the public paying the bill for an exhorbitant settlement after the rigors of a tie-up in which it has been the prime sufferer.

Lowenberg [9] studied the contract negotiations of police and fire fighters under a compulsory arbitration law. He found that "the availability of compulsory arbitration did not terminate collective bargaining activity among police and fire fighters in Pennsylvania." Two-thirds of the municipalities discussed in the article arrived at a negotiated settlement. In addition, he found that "evidence exists that arbitration was used at times as a tactical weapon by both sides, rather than as a court of last resort to resolve a deadlock in bargaining." He concluded that "despite

employer objections to arbitration awards and some employee
unhappiness with particular awards, compulsory arbitration seemed
to fulfill its major purpose in 1968, i.e., to provide an alternative
to strike action as a terminal point in collective bargaining."

Having listed some arguments for and against compulsory
arbitration in general, we discuss below the pros and cons of
different types of compulsory arbitration, beginning with voluntary
arbitration. The National Electrical Contractors Association and
The International Brotherhood of Electrical Workers have a
Council on Industrial Relations that serves as a court in labor-
management disputes [10]. The twelve-man council has been in
existence since 1920. About 90 per cent of the IBEW locals have a
"council clause" in their contracts. Disputes that cannot be solved
must be submitted to the council. Strikes and lockouts are barred.
The electrical contracting business has experienced success with
this system, but could it be successful in other industries? Probably
not in its exact form unless conditions are similar to those in
construction [10]. Bargaining in the construction industry is
almost always limited to local contracts. Clashes generally involve
local issues, personalities, and animosities. The council can smooth
over these differences by establishing a common bargain that fits
precedents [10]. "It would be hard to do this in mass production
industries or . . . the transportation industry. National bargaining
and national patterns are too pronounced [10]." Since we are
concerned with public sector and critical industries, this type of
voluntary arbitration would not serve our purpose.

Many of the drawbacks inherent in compulsory arbitration are
circumvented in an ingenious arbitration procedure proposed by
Stevens [7]. He proposed a "one-or-the-other" method by which
the arbitrator would make his award. The arbitrator is required to
choose the last offer of one or the other parties. This requirement
would force both parties to compromise and concede points before
making their last offer. This would be for fear that the arbitrator
would choose the last offer of the opponent because it was more
reasonable. Therefore, the "one-or-the-other" method of arbitration
would generate the same uncertainties and fears of costs to the
opponents that an impending strike does. This would lead to
concessions and compromise and, therefore, maintain viable collective bargaining even under compulsory arbitration. The Stevens
method should answer the criticism by Schwartz that compulsory
arbitration would end all collective bargaining negotiations. A
related argument by Denise, that the parties would hold back their

best offer, is also answered. Another complaint about compulsory arbitration is that it will lead to both parties making a large number of demands. Since the arbitrator is not intimately acquainted with the parties, they may present demands that an insider would consider ludicrous. The extra demands also leave the arbitrator with room to maneuver. This argument carries no weight under the "one-or-the-other" method because the parties would be very reluctant to include superfluous demands. The reason is that the superfluous demands might weigh down the final offer package and force the arbitrator to choose the final offer package from the other party. The "one-or-the-other" method proposed by Stevens is undoubtedly a major step toward a workable compulsory arbitration method.

Foster [11] has reservations about the Stevens method and pointed to several shortcomings. He answered the premise that the Stevens method introduces the uncertainty inherent in a possible strike. He says that the real danger is that it introduces an element of gamesmanship that may hinder the search for accommodation. The negotiator may consider the situation more of a challenge than a threat. In regard to the uncertainty factor, he believes that each of the negotiators will move toward a point that they feel the arbitrator will approve. If they both predict the same point, they may very well agree before arbitration. But if their predictions are different, they will probably stop before reaching agreement. The odds of this occurrence are greatest with vague criteria for arbitration decisions. Therefore, the criteria should be as explicit as possible. Another problem, he believes, is that strikes may occur even though they are illegal. If the management package is accepted as most reasonable, the arbitrator is bound by law not to add any labor "sweeteners." This could lead to strikes. While the inflexibility of the Stevens method is what invites bargaining, it also invites defiance if bargaining breaks down. Foster's arguments deserve serious consideration when searching for a viable compulsory arbitration method.

Garber [12] also feels there are drawbacks to the Stevens method. Due to the total-package concept, the arbitrator has too little flexibility. The arbitrator may be faced with a situation in which the overall package is more reasonable and yet contains one demand that is totally unreasonable. Garber proposed a five-step plan under which "the arbitration panel would be obligated to choose the 'most reasonable' of the parties' last offers for each disputed issue" [12]. The steps are:

1. The parties would choose an arbitration panel from a prescribed list. If unable to agree, a panel would be selected for them by the appeal board.
2. A preliminary hearing would be held to determine the issues to be discussed and the procedures to be employed.
3. The arbitration hearing would be held, during which, the parties would present their last offer for each disputed issue and their reasons for stating why the offers are reasonable. The panel would make its decision based on specified criteria and supply a defense of its decision.
4. Either of the parties would be allowed to appeal the decision to the appeal board. Appeal to the courts would be allowed under specified conditions.
5. The decisions of the panel, subject to appeals to the appeal board, would be implemented. Appeals to the courts would not block implementation.

Garber called his method "last-offer arbitration." He pointed out that his method gives the arbitrator more flexibility than the Stevens method while retaining the same amount of risk. However, he acknowledged that unlike the Stevens method under which the parties might forfeit their unimportant demands for fear of weighing down their packages, the last-offer procedure may encourage these unimportant issues to be tacked on. Garber feels that his proposed system will still lead to better results than the Stevens system despite this one drawback.

One criticism of compulsory arbitration is that it is virtually costless. Since the costs of the process will not tax either the union's or the company's treasury, both sides are willing to go to arbitration over even minor issues. Neal Chamberlain [1] proposed to charge the parties for the services of the arbitration machinery. The parties would be assessed a cost per day based on the number of members in the union or the assets of the company. This is an intriguing idea if a method can be worked out for deciding upon a fair assessment for the parties. Assessing labor and management the same costs probably would not work because three million dollars out of the United Steelworkers' treasury would probably do more damage than three million dollars out of U.S. Steel's treasury. If the cost were calculated based on what a strike would cost, then the question arises as to whether you assume the company has adequate inventory to coast through several months of strike without loss of revenue. If an equitable method could be developed for calculating these costs, then utilization of the

Chamberlain method might cut down on the arbitration load and lead to a more efficient system.

So far we have discussed the pros and cons of compulsory arbitration and several proposed methods. The majority of experts in labor relations, at first, dismissed the idea of compulsory arbitration without discussion. Stevens [7] presented the current status of compulsory arbitration very well:

> In addition to these indications of a need for a thaw in heretofore frozen attitudes about compulsory arbitration, the increasing frequency of professional discussion of the issue suggests that the "law of the propagation of heretical doctrines" may be at work. If the initial proponents of such a doctrine (i.e., that resort to compulsory arbitration is not *prima facie* death knell for the free enterprise system) are not forthwith struck down by Jovian bolts, then other investigators may be inclined to give the matter serious attention.

Now that different types of compulsory arbitration have been discussed, a return will be made to the subject of compulsory arbitration in general. The case for compulsory arbitration is very simple. David Straus, former President of American Arbitration said, "If labor and management are incapable of reaching agreement through free collective bargaining in major negotiations which affect our economy, then in the end some collective bargaining will be called a failure, and some form of government controls will take over" [3]. Even those who propose methods of compulsory arbitration hope that management and labor will be able to reach agreement without governmental controls. A faint ray of hope in this area appeared during the 1967 contract negotiations in the steel industry. The top union leadership presented the top policy-making board of the United Steelworkers of America with a voluntary arbitration plan. The plan had emerged from a meeting between the union officers and the four-man steel industry bargaining team. The plan called for labor and management to bargain for approximately 60 days and then decide on which remaining issues would be submitted to binding arbitration. If the parties could not agree, the document called for all issues to be arbitrated while the parties surrendered the right to strike and lockout. The proposal had already been approved by management [13]. The union leaders were split over the proposal, and they later rejected it; however, I. W. Abel, President of the United Steelworkers said he did not close the door to possible future agreements of this kind [14]. The plan with modifications was later approved by the steel industry.

One of the prime arguments against compulsory arbitration is that the British tried it and later abolished it. McKelvey [15] studied the British system and stated that one of the problems with the system was that the arbitration board did not explain its decisions. This led to uncertainty as to how future disputes should be treated. This problem is eliminated in the last offer method because of the requirement that the arbitration board must explain its decisions. An argument for compulsory arbitration is that the Australians use the system and their unions are stronger than American unions [4].

In conclusion, it is felt that some form of compulsory arbitration should be legislated as a last step in negotiations in the public and critical sectors. Our society can no longer tolerate work stoppages in critical industries such as steel and transportation. The losses in freedom for management and unions must be balanced against the increased freedom of our society to receive an uninterrupted supply of critical goods and services. There are drawbacks to every form of compulsory arbitration thus far proposed. Cullen [1] stated that "it must be clear that one of the easiest parlor games imaginable is puncturing other peoples' ideas for handling emergency strikes." It is the authors' opinion that the most viable compulsory arbitration procedure is the last-offer method of Garber. The procedure could possibly be improved by charging the parties for the arbitration process as proposed by Chamberlain. First, however, an equitable means must be found for assessing the costs. The major problem with any form of governmental control of strikes is compliance. Cullen [1] asserted that "the evidence is perfectly clear that American unions and employers will comply with most strike controls most of the time, but that every control will sooner or later be violated by someone." However, it is believed that compulsory arbitration in the public and critical sector will lead to less industrial strife than the present system.

## REFERENCES

1. Donald E. Cullen, *National Emergency Strikes*, Cornell Univ., Ithaca, New York; 1968.
2. Orme W. Phelps, "Compulsory Arbitration: Some Perspectives," *Industrial and Labor Relations*, XVIII (Oct. 1964), pp. 81. XVII, 81, October, 1964.
3. Walter G. Seinsheimer, "What's So Terrible about Compulsory Arbitration?" *The Arbitration Journal*, XXVI (April 1971), pp. 220. XXVI, 220, April, 1971.
4. Brotherhood of Railroad Trainmen, *The Pros and Cons of Compulsory Arbitration* BRT, Cleveland, Ohio, 1965.

5. A. H. Raskin, "Labor's Crisis of Public Confidence," *Saturday Review*, March 30, 1963.
6. Asher M. Schwartz, "Is Compulsory Arbitration Necessary," *The Arbitration Journal*, XV 1960,.
7. Carl M. Stevens, "Is Compulsory Arbitration Compatible with Bargaining?" *Industrial Relations*, V Feb., 1966.
8. Malcolm L. Denise, "On the Effect of Arbitration on Labor-Management Relations," *The Arbitration Journal*, VII 1952.
9. Joseph J. Lowenberg, "Compulsory Arbitration for Police and Fire Fighters in Pennsylvania in 1968," *Industrial and Labor Relations Review*, XXIII April, 1970.
10. "How to Stop Strikes—Before They Start," *Business Week*, Aug. 24, 1963.
11. Howard G. Foster, "Final Offer Selection in National Emergency Disputes," *The Arbitration Journal*, XXVII 1972.
12. Philip E. Garber, "Compulsory Arbitration in the Public Sector: A Proposed Alternative," *The Arbitration Journal*, 1971.
13. "Steel Union Split Over Arbitration," *NY Times*, Oct. 27, 1967.
14. "Steelworkers Veto No Strike Proposal for '68 Labor Talks," *Wall Street Journal*, Dec. 4, 1967.
15. Jean Trepp McKelvey, "Compulsory Arbitration of Labor Disputes in Great Britain," *The Arbitration Journal*, VII 1952.

\*              \*              \*

Dr. L. Bruce McDonald is currently a Human Factors Specialist in the Engineering Sciences Division of Midwest Research Institute In Kansas City, Missouri. He was formerlly associated with the LTV Aerospace Corporation in Dallas as a human factors engineer.

Dr. M.J. Fox Jr. P.E. is an Associate Professor of Industrial Engineering at Texas A&M University. He also serves on the Labor Arbitration Panels of the American Arbitration Association and the Federal Mediation and Conciliation Service. Dr. Fox has published extensively in the fields relating to labor relations.

## Discussion Questions

1. How have technological changes in industry and government affected the propensity of unions to strike?
2. Discuss some of the arguments against compulsory arbitration. How valid are they?
3. Do you believe that a third party can understand the positions, motives, and needs of the two parties to a dispute and render a "fair" decision?

*Reprinted from Journal of Collective Negotiations in the Public Sector, Fall, 1974*

# CHAPTER 6

# Compulsory Arbitration Versus Negotiations for Public Safety Employees: The Michigan Experience

**ROBERT H. BEZDEK**
*Bureau of Economic Analysis*
*U.S. Department of Commerce*
*Washington, D.C.*

**DAVID W. RIPLEY**
*Institute of Labor and Industrial Relations*
*University of Illinois, Urbana*

In the past decade public employees have become increasingly militant. To deal with strikes, slowdowns, sick-outs, and other job actions by public employees—especially police and firefighters—local governments have turned to compulsory arbitration in an effort to treat unions equitably while at the same time preventing the disruption of essential public services. One of the most frequent criticisms of compulsory arbitration in the public sector is that this method of dispute settlement, by shifting the responsibility for the settlement from public officials to the arbitration panel, tends to result in settlement awards larger than would otherwise be agreed to and often larger than the municipalities can afford to pay.[1] Here we investigate this important issue by analyzing the Michigan experience with compulsory arbitration for police and firefighters in the late 1960's and early 1970's. Our results indicate that, contrary to popular belief, compulsory arbitration does not lead to wage increases for government employees which are larger than those resulting from other methods of dispute settlement.

## Background

In 1965 the State of Michigan enacted the Public Employment Relations Act, the first statute in two decades that dealt with public employee relations [2]. This act retained previous laws' provisions prohibiting public employee strikes but did grant government workers several other rights of unionization. These new rights included permission for public employees regardless of level in government to join labor unions or other organizations for the purpose of collective bargaining free of employer restraint, the right of exclusive representation, and the right to engage in collective bargaining with respect to the terms and conditions of employment.

The enactment of this new statute quickly led to widespread organizing activity by labor organizations seeking to represent the now eligible public employees. Along with the increased union activity came a rash of public employee strikes and sick-outs, and in the late 1960's Michigan led the nation in the number of occurrences of voluntary public employee work stoppages [3]. Included in these work stoppages were a number of serious ones involving the vital public safety areas of law enforcement and fire protection. In an attempt to cope with this alarming situation the Michigan State Legislature in 1969 passed Public Act 312 on Police and Firemen's Arbitration (hereafter referred to as Public Act 312) to determine whether compulsory arbitration was a viable solution to impasse resolution within the public sector [4]. This act was based on the premise that:

> Since the right to strike is legally denied and cannot be realistically conferred on employees engaged in vital services, then a substitute bargaining balancer, the right to invoke binding arbitration by a mutual third party, is an effective and equitable substitute as a dispute settlement procedure [5].

[1] For a recent discussion of the issues involved in compulsory arbitration for public safety employees, see Wortman and Overton [1].

Michigan thus became the fourth state, after Wyoming in 1965 and Pennsylvania and Rhode Island in 1968, to enact legislation requiring compulsory arbitration of labor disputes involving police and firefighters.[2]

Michigan's Public Act 312 was unique in several respects. First of all, it was the only compulsory arbitration statute specifically adopted on a trial basis, and it was slated to expire on June 30, 1972, unless extended by the legislature. Secondly, this Act was the first state compulsory arbitration statute calling for both mediation and fact finding before petitions for compulsory arbitration could be filed. This provision enhanced the likelihood that meaningful collective bargaining would occur before an impasse developed. Finally, Public Act 312 contained comprehensive criteria that were to be considered by arbitrators in their deliberations, and the legislature included these criteria to insure that arbitrators would not exceed delegated authority.

In May 1972 the State legislature extended the provisions of Public Act 312 through June 30, 1975, over the determined opposition of many interest groups. In the spring of 1972 bills were introduced in the legislature to both repeal the Act and to revise it substantially, and lobbying efforts were intense on behalf of both proponents and opponents of its extension. Extension of the Act was strongly supported by the Police Officers Association of Michigan, Michigan firefighters, and the Michigan AFL-CIO and other labor organizations. Opposition to the extension of Public Act 312 was lead by the Michigan Municipal League and the Michigan Public Personnel Association.

The main reason the Public Personnel Association and the Municipal League favored repeal of the Act centered on the "ability to pay" issue. Ability to pay the economic awards decided upon by a majority of the arbitration panel was one of the ten criteria listed in Public Act 312 that were to be considered by arbitrators in awarding settlements. These two organizations felt that ability to pay criteria had not been given sufficient weight by arbitrators and that most of the settlements under this act had been too high—especially in the area of wage increases. In a position paper advocating repeal of Public Act 312, the Municipal League [6] stated:

> Despite the insertion in the legislation of standards to guide arbitrators in resolving disputes, including the admonition to consider the ability of the government to meet the costs involved, arbitrators in the cases thus far have frequently dismissed or minimized consideration of ability to pay. In a

---

[2] The Wyoming statute covered firefighters only.

majority of the arbitration awards the amount of the pay increase awarded has been excessive in comparison with pay increases established through negotiations.

Here we examine the important question of whether, in general, wage increases granted under compulsory arbitration statutes tend to be higher than those resulting from other dispute settlement procedures. Specifically, we investigate whether the salary increases received by Michigan police officers and firefighters under compulsory arbitration between 1969 and 1972 were higher than those obtained by policemen and firemen in this state through negotiations during the same period.

## Empirical Analysis

The precise number of police and firefighters' bargaining units subject to Public Act 312 is unknown, but is estimated to lie between 500 and 600 units [7]. In the first three years of the Act well over 100 cases involving police and firefighters were submitted to binding arbitration because negotiations, mediation, and fact-finding efforts by the Michigan Employment Relations Commission had failed to resolve the impasses [8]. Of these cases, half were settled by awards rendered by state appointed compulsory arbitration panels, one-third were still pending at the time the data for our study were collected, and the remainder were either settled privately or were withdrawn before a compulsory arbitration hearing could be conducted. Of the arbitration awards studied only those involving 28 cities could be analyzed here.[3] As a control group we selected 18 cities that had settled similar contract disputes through negotiations during the same period. The total size of our sample was thus 46 cities.

Here we wished to use both minimum and maximum salaries to determine whether the benefits awarded under compulsory arbitration were significantly higher than those determined through collective negotiations. To avoid problems of regional comparability, in our analysis we utilized the Michigan Municipal League's three regional divisions. These state regions consist of the Detroit Metropolitan area, the southern one-half of the lower peninsula (excluding those cities within the Detroit Metropolitan area), and the remainder of the state. Of the 46 cities in the sample, 27 were in the

---

[3] The data pertaining to the arbitration awards in the other cities were not sufficient to allow us to include these awards in our analysis.

Detroit Metropolitan area, 13 were in southern lower Michigan, and 6 were in the northern part of the state.

We used analysis of variance to test the null hypothesis that the minimum and the maximum salaries determined through compulsory arbitration were equal to the minimum and maximum salaries determined through collective negotiation. We used a 2-by-3-by-2 factorial design that contained no nesting among independent variables. The independent variables were compulsory arbitration—collective negotiations (factor A), geographical areas: metropolitan, northern and southern (factor B) and policemen-firefighters (factor C).[4]

Table 1 summarizes the results of our analysis of variance tests for minimum and maximum salaries. Considering the results for minimum salaries first, the table shows that neither the second-order interactions (A × B × C) nor the first-order interactions (A × B, B × C, A × C) were significant. The main effects for factor A (compulsory arbitration—collective negotiations) and factor C (policemen—firefighters) were not significant either. As anticipated, however, factor B—geographical region—was highly significant, with an F ratio of 101.13. The results for maximum salaries summarized in the table present a similar picture. Once again, neither the second order interaction (A × B × C) nor the first order interactions (A × B, B × C, A × C) were significant. The main effect for factor A (compulsory arbitration-collective negotiations) was not significant, although the main effect for factor C (police and firefighters) was significant. Again, as expected, factor B, geographical region, was highly significant with an F ratio of 180.9. Our null hypothesis was thus accepted and, in sum, our findings here indicated that there was no statistically significant difference between the police and firefighters' salaries awarded under the compulsory arbitration procedures specified in Public Act 312 and those determined through collective negotiations.

Our analysis concerned only mean police and firefighters salaries; however, in an unpublished study utilizing the same basic data, Philip Morilanen and Kent Mudie [7] compared the rates of increase of police and firefighters salaries determined under compulsory arbitration and under collective negotiations with the rates of increase the

---

[4] Because the factorial design was not balanced and contained an unequal number of observations per cell, the results of our analysis of varience tests cannot be entirely precise. For a discussion of this problem see Blalock [9] or a comparable statistics text.

Table 1. Analysis of Variance Summary Table for Minimum and Maximum Salaries

| Source | Sum of Squares | | Degrees of Freedom | | Mean Square | | F Ratio | |
|---|---|---|---|---|---|---|---|---|
| | Min | Max | Min | Max | Min | Max | Min | Max |
| Factor A | .2714 06 | .1388 05 | 1 | 1 | .2714 06 | .1388 05 | 0.6689 | 0.0319 |
| Factor B | .8208 08 | .1575 09 | 2 | 2 | .4104 08 | .7878 08 | 101.1299[b] | 180.940 [b] |
| Factor C | .1278 07 | .2436 07 | 1 | 1 | .1278 07 | .2436 07 | 3.1496 | 5.5957[a] |
| A X B | .3658 06 | .3316 04 | 2 | 2 | .1829 06 | .1658 04 | 0.4508 | 0.0038 |
| A X C | .3340 06 | .4834 06 | 1 | 1 | .3340 06 | .4834 06 | 0.8231 | 1.1103 |
| B X C | .4545 06 | .3893 06 | 2 | 2 | .2272 06 | .7786 06 | 0.5600 | 0.8941 |
| A X B X C | .8039 06 | .7339 06 | 2 | 2 | .4019 06 | .3669 06 | 0.9905 | 0.8427 |
| Error | .2597 08 | .3135 08 | 64 | 72 | .4058 06 | .4354 06 | | |

[a] $p < .001$
[b] $p < .05$

Table 2. Rates of Salary Increases Determined Under Compulsory
Arbitration and Collective Negotiations

|  |  | Compulsory arbitration % | Collective negotiations % |
|---|---|---|---|
| Police | Region 1 | 12.68 | 12.66 |
|  | Region 2 | 10.03 | 9.77 |
|  | Region 3 | 6.6 | 12.19 |
| Firefighters | Region 1 | 12.19 | 11.34 |
|  | Region 2 | 7.0 | 6.97 |
|  | Region 3 | 12.82 | 8.16 |

Source: Morilanen and Mudie [7].

cities had granted in previous years. Table 2 summarizes the
Morilanen and Mudie findings and illustrates that there was no
noticeable difference between the rates of salary increase granted
under compulsory arbitration and those obtained through collective
negotiations. Morilanen and Mudie [10] also reported that in over
two-thirds of the cases studied the rate of salary increase granted by
the arbitration panel was less than the rate of salary increase the city
had granted at least once in the previous three years.

The results of our study, taken in conjunction with the findings
derived by Morilanen and Mudie, thus strongly indicate that the
Michigan police and firefighters' salaries determined through compulsory arbitration between 1969 and 1972 and those collectively
negotiated over the same period were not significantly different in
terms of mean salaries or rates of salary increase. This point is
illustrated even more clearly in Table 3, which shows the minimum
and maximum mean salary second order interaction (A X B X C).
This table shows that both the minimum and maximum police
salaries determined under compulsory arbitration (with the exception of maximum salary in the Detroit Metropolitan area) were all
lower than those determined through collective negotiations.
Compulsory arbitration awards involving firefighters' salaries in the
Detroit area are also seen to have been lower. In the southern and
northern state regions a reversal occurred, with the compulsory
arbitration salary awards being higher for both minimum and
maximum salaries. A comparison of firefighters salaries with their
police counterparts in these areas explains this situation. Arbitrators
apparently awarded higher salaries to the firefighters in those areas to

Table 3. Means of A X B X C Interaction

| A X B X C interaction | Mean minimum salary* | Mean maximum salary* |
|---|---|---|
| Negotiations, metro, police | $9,830 | $11,500 |
| Arbitration, metro, police | 9,597 | 11,608 |
| Negotiations, metro, fireman | 9,797 | 11,416 |
| Arbitration, metro, fireman | 9,197 | 11,225 |
| Negotiationa, South, police | 8,380 | 9,656 |
| Arbitration, South, Police | 7,827 | 9,297 |
| Negotiations, South, Fireman | 7,716 | 8,990 |
| Arbitration, South, Fireman | 8,125 | 9,327 |
| Negotiations, North, Police | 6,644 | 7,579 |
| Arbitration, North, Police | 6,421 | 7,116 |
| Negotiations, North, Fireman | 5,777 | 6,347 |
| Arbitration, North, Fireman | 6,018 | 6,709 |

*Salaries rounded to nearest dollar.

achieve the salary parity that already existed between policemen and firemen in the rest of the state. On the whole, however, compulsory arbitration awards appeared to be somewhat lower than those established through collective negotiations.

## Conclusions and Implications for Further Research

Here we were concerned with a critical problem of public sector labor relations: whether compulsory arbitration offers a viable grievance settlement for policemen, firemen, and other public employees performing vital services. Using the recent Michigan experience with Public Act 312, which provided for compulsory arbitration of labor disputes involving police and firefighters, we investigated whether the awards granted by the state appointed arbitrators were higher than those determined under collective negotiations in the period 1969-1972. Our findings, coupled with the results of a recently completed study by Philip Morilanen and Kent Mudie, clearly contradict the widespread belief that settlements awarded under compulsory arbitration are higher than those arrived at by other means of dispute settlement. In Michigan it was seen that the apparent difference in the awards was due to the arbitrators' desire to achieve greater statewide equalization of police and firefighters' salaries. The fears of Michigan municipal organizations concerning the extension of the Act to 1975 were thus groundless.

We do not claim that our findings reported here are entirely conclusive. Obviously, our analysis concerned dispute settlement only for policemen and firemen in the State of Michigan over a relatively short period of time, and we have no way of determining if our conclusions would apply to the situations in other states. One problem which should be noted here is that Public Act 312 mandated compulsory arbitration for deadlocked public labor disputes, and this may have had some influence in encouraging higher awards in those cases settled through collective negotiations. Another problem concerns the use of salary as the sole variable in our analysis, and a more comprehensive investigation would require the costing-out of the value of the entire settlement package. Unfortunately, information on fringe benefits such as gun, food, clothing and cleaning allowances, health and life insurance benefits, and holiday, vacation, and overtime pay were computed in dollar terms by very few of the municipalities involved in this study, and no arbitration panel reported being presented with data on fringe benefits. We therefore had no option but to ignore the issue of fringe benefits in our study.

Further research is thus called for to investigate the size of the awards resulting from compulsory arbitration relative to those arrived at through other means of public sector dispute settlement in different regions of the nation. If possible, care should be taken to include in the analysis the entire cost of the settlement package. Nevertheless, the findings reported here indicate that compulsory arbitration awards are not larger than those established through negotiations, and this conclusion has important implications for the potential of compulsory arbitration as a solution to impasse resolution within the public sector.

## REFERENCES

1. Max S. Wortman and Craig E. Overton, "Compulsory Arbitration: The End of the Line in the Police Field?" *Public Personnel Management*, Vol. 2, pp. 4-8, January-February, 1973.
2. Doris B. McLaughlin, *Michigan Labor: A Brief History*, p. 148, University of Michigan Press, Ann Arbor, 1970.
3. U.S. Department of Labor, Bureau of Labor Statistics, *Work Stoppages in Government, 1958-1968*, BLS Report 348, p. 15, Washington, D.C., 1970.
4. Bureau of National Affairs, "Public Employment Relations Act," *Government Employee Relations Report*, 51: 3111-3115, 1972.
5. Arvid Anderson, "Compulsory Arbitration in Public Sector Dispute Settlement—An Affirmative View," *Industrial Relations Research Association, Proceedings*, p. 5, 1971.

6. Michigan Municipal League, *Position Paper Regarding the Compulsory Arbitration of Municipal Police and Fire Labor Disputes*, p. 2-3, Detroit, 1972.
7. Philip M. Morilanen and Kent W. Mudie, "Compulsory Arbitration in Michigan," unpublished report, p. 9, University of Michigan, Ann Arbor, Michigan, 1972.
8. Michigan State Senate Labor Committee, *A Review of Compulsory Arbitration in Michigan*, p. 2, Ann Arbor, Michigan, 1972.
9. Hubert M. Blalock, *Social Statistics*, McGraw-Hill, New York, 1972.
10. Morilanen and Mudie, p. 16.

\*         \*         \*

Roger H. Bezdek is a senior economist in the Bureau of Economic Analysis of the U.S. Department of Commerce, David W. Ripley is a graduate student in the Institute of Labor and Industrial Relations, University of Illinois at Urbana-Champaign. This research was conducted while Dr. Bezdek was a member of the faculty of the University of Illinois.

## Discussion Questions

1. Should "job actions" among essential public employees be treated as severely as strikes? Why, or why not?
2. Why might wage increases granted under compulsory arbitration laws tend to be higher than those resulting from other resolution techniques?
3. Discuss the concept of parity on a local and statewide basis from the point of view of unions, governments, and taxpayers.

*Reprinted from Journal of Collective Negotiations in the Public Sector, Spring, 1974*

# CHAPTER 7

# *The Effect of Compulsory Arbitration on Collective Negotiations*

**J. JOSEPH LOEWENBERG**
*Associate Professor*
*Temple University*

## Introduction

In the last few years, a dictum of labor relations has been questioned seriously and, to some minds, become suspect. The dictum is that compulsory arbitration and collective bargaining are incompatible. This article will review the traditional arguments and evidence and then analyze the renewed interest in and recent experience with compulsory arbitration. Finally, the article will offer some suggestions about structuring compulsory arbitration.

## The Case Against Compulsory Arbitration

Much has been written on the detrimental effect of compulsory arbitration as a method of impasse resolution on collective bargaining [1]. The principal arguments emphasize the process and results of compulsory arbitration [2].

Collective bargaining is essentially a legislative process whereby union and management attempt to arrive at the terms of a new agreement by resolving their differences. The process is one of compromise, but only those affected by the outcome can determine the precise nature of the give-and-take. In compulsory arbitration, on the other hand, a third party intervenes to determine judicially the terms of the agreement. Since each party realizes that the negotiations may terminate in compulsory arbitration, each side is reluctant to change its initial position, lest the change place that side at a disadvantage in arbitration. Consequently, the availability of compulsory arbitration tends to freeze the parties in their respective initial positions and forestall meaningful collective bargaining.

A major attribute of collective bargaining is that the negotiators assume responsibility for the results and are motivated to interpret the terms of the agreement in accordance with the negotiations. Compulsory arbitration permits both parties to escape responsibility for the final terms. If the award is unpopular with constituents, leaders on either side may blame the arbitrator. Moreover, neither party will necessarily feel responsible for administration of contract terms that it did not agree to. As a result, compulsory arbitration leads to chaos in the bargaining relationship between union and management.

Because the parties are not committed to either the process or the results of compulsory arbitration, and because compulsory arbitration weakens the ties between the leaders and followers on each side as well as the relationship between the parties, compulsory arbitration leads to the very thing it is supposed to prevent: strikes. The practical and legal problems of ending strikes are not diminished by providing for compulsory arbitration.

The longest and most widespread use of compulsory arbitration has been in Australia. The experience of more than half a century has not been favorable in promoting collective bargaining or in ending strikes [3]. Compulsory arbitration was originally adopted to assist weak unions in bargaining collectively with employers and to end wasteful strikes. Only unions which registered with the authorities were subject to compulsory arbitration, but most unions have registered. While unions have indeed become stronger—much stronger than employers, according to some analysts—neither collective bargaining nor a cessation of stoppages has resulted. The parties have come to rely so on the arbitration system that they are unwilling and unable to bargain. The Australian labor relations picture has become the classic illustration of those who argue the case against compulsory arbitration.

## The Case for Compulsory Arbitration [4]

Despite the authoritative verdict against compulsory arbitration, interest in the subject has again emerged on both theoretical and practical levels. The revived interest indicates that the final word regarding the effect of compulsory arbitration on collective bargaining remains to be spoken.

The proponents for reevaluating the place of compulsory arbitration in collective bargaining point to the areas where compulsory arbitration is already in effect and considered desirable, namely in grievance procedures and in representation and unfair labor cases within the jurisdiction of the National Labor Relations Board or similar administrative agencies. To be sure, such cases are not identical to contract negotiations. However, the differences between interests and rights of the parties are not always clear-cut. Moreover, the types of situations already subject to compulsory arbitration may sometimes be more significant for union-management relations than many subjects raised in contract negotiations.

The existence of compulsory arbitration in the above areas has *not* resulted in the automatic invocation of compulsory arbitration. Most cases involving grievances and representation issues have been decided by the parties, though sometimes with the assistance of an outside person. Moreover, some cases have been referred to arbitration for political reasons and as face-saving measures rather than because of a deadlock in negotiations, without irreparably damaging the integrity of the procedure of collective bargaining.

The scope of the compulsory arbitration award in contract negotiation impasses is limited by the terms of submission, the composition of the tribunal, the existing agreement and proposals of the parties, and the normal criteria applied in negotiations by the parties themselves. Where compulsory arbitration has been used in contract negotiations, such as in wartime or other emergency situations, research indicates that the results of arbitration are close to what the parties themselves might have settled on.

Under given conditions compulsory arbitration may serve much the same purpose as a strike [5]. The purpose of a strike

and/or lockout is to provide each part of the negotiations with a
vehicle for imposing a cost on the other side if the other side is
unwilling to agree to its proposals. The threat of this cost—or
the actual cost, if the threat is carried out—puts pressure on
both sides to negotiate within a set framework of differences.
The purpose of compulsory arbitration could be the same as
that of the strike, i.e., to encourage the parties to negotiate
within a "contract zone." In the case of both the strike and
compulsory arbitration, the degree to which negotiations are
fostered depends upon the parties' expectations of the outcome.
While all forms of compulsory arbitration may not lead to the
same goal, there is no reason why this instrument cannot be
fashioned to produce the desired result and thus make it an
acceptable alternative to the strike in collective bargaining.

This type of thinking seems to have been applied in the case
of Canada's Public Service Staff Relations Act of 1967 [6]. Before
the start of each round of bargaining, the employees' bargaining
agent must choose whether any dispute resulting from that
negotiation will be settled by strike or arbitration procedures.
Interestingly enough, in the first four years of the act the
overwhelming majority of employees had selected arbitration,
yet only three agreements were actually decided by arbitration.
Admittedly, this procedure is not quite compulsory arbitration
since the employee bargaining agent may always opt out; in only
four units has a switch occurred, two which had originally
elected compulsory arbitration later choosing the option to
strike, and two moving in the other direction [7].

In the United States, too, experience with compulsory
arbitration has been mounting. Minnesota has provided compulsory arbitration for labor relations disputes in private and
nonprofit hospitals since 1947; less than 15 per cent of the
settlements have been determined in arbitration. As of Summer
1971, six states had introduced compulsory arbitration as the
binding method of settling bargaining disputes between public
employers and their police and/or firefighters [8]. The motivation
for introducing compulsory arbitration has been fear of illegal
stoppages in essential services and the ineffectiveness of traditional methods, including fact finding, to prevent such stoppages. Although the experience under these laws is too recent to
be conclusive, it suggests that compulsory arbitration does not
impair collective bargaining immediately, but that it does curtail
strikes and other forms of work stoppages.

## Conditions for Compulsory Arbitration

A closer look at some of the main factors contributing to the use and early success of compulsory arbitration in the United States may suggest the conditions and limitations of compulsory arbitration as a means of resolving labor relations disputes.

### AFFECTED PORTION OF THE ECONOMY

Compulsory arbitration is currently available to few workers, although Mayor John V. Lindsay recently signed legislation providing compulsory binding arbitration for New York City municipal employees (exempting teachers and Transit Authority employees). If all workers in the occupational groups for whom compulsory arbitration is available in some states were accorded the same procedure, the proportion of these workers to the total civilian labor force would still be small. All police, firefighters and hospital personnel constitute about 4 per cent of the employed civilian labor force. Two consequences follow from this fact. First, even if all affected employees made use of compulsory arbitration, arbitrators would still have many reference points outside of compulsory awards on which to determine their findings. A closed system in which all conditions would be based on other arbitrated conditions could threaten to become unrealistic to market conditions. This danger is avoided when compulsory arbitration is available only to a small portion of the total work force. Second, the value of arbitrated awards is but a fraction of the total package of national wages and conditions. The arbitration system is therefore under less pressure and more acceptable than if it were applicable to all workers involved in collective bargaining. This conclusion does not mean to ignore the relationship between arbitrated wages and other wages in the system; for instance, an increase in police wages will affect the wages of other employees in the same political jurisdiction. The conclusion recognizes, however, a difference in the way in which such wages and working conditions are determined and the diminishing effect of arbitration decisions in other wage clusters and bargaining structures.

### EMPLOYEE CHARACTERISTICS

The employees for whom compulsory arbitration has been made available as a terminal point to collective bargaining procedures share some common characteristics. These characteristics in part account for their having compulsory arbitration and in part contribute to their acceptance of compulsory arbitration as a terminal procedure.

In a functional sense, the employees feel they are professional workers, or at least a part of a professional team. Indeed, the stress on professionalism is growing for police and firefighters and for those hospital workers who have previously not regarded themselves as professionals. Even for the latter group, the identity with a professional team effort is greater than for similar occupational groups in other environments.

The employees regard themselves—and, in turn, are regarded by the rest of the community—as performing work essential to the well-being of the community. Disruption in the service would do serious damage. Continued performance of service is a recognized social contribution on which the employees can pride themselves. (This is not to say that disruptions in service cannot take place, but the workers are loathe to take such a step, both because of the actual effect and because it will damage their reputation for performing an essential service.)

Closely related to the above point is the tradition among the employees not to engage in pressure tactics. For certain of these employees, this tradition has for long periods been formalized and reinforced in the constitutions of their representative organizations. The elimination of bans on pressure tactics may reflect some weakening of traditional attitudes, but it also represents a more flexible strategy as much as a new eagerness to strike.

## EMPLOYER CHARACTERISTICS

The only group of employers thus far involved in compulsory arbitration in the United States are public and (in Minnesota hospitals) nonprofit private employers. The limitation of compulsory arbitration to this group of employers is significant, because such employers operate under different pressures in bargaining than do employers in the private sector [9]. The latter are ultimately concerned with the effects of the bargaining process and the product of bargaining on their financial positions. The former are not concerned with financial implications in and of themselves. Higher costs due to increased wages, lowered efficiency, or other reasons are acceptable as long as there are no political repercussions. Only when the electorate (in the case of the public employer) or the board of directors (in the case of the nonprofit employer) hold the employer directly accountable for unacceptably higher costs are the financial effects significant. This usually occurs when the price of services must be raised in the form of new taxes, or charges to consumer subsidies—and when the employer's actions have contributed directly to the rise. If external factors produced the cost rise, the employer can usually escape the repercussions, unlike his counterpart in the private sector.

The potential employer weapon of traditional collective bargaining—economic power as expressed in the ability to lock out—is inapplicable in the case of public employers. Such employers do not have the power, politically or practically, to lock out employees. When the employees involved are considered essential to public health and safety, the possibility of taking a strike is further removed.

Other aspects that may distinguish between employers in the public/nonprofit sector and employers in the private sector are division of authority, which makes more difficult attributing responsibility for decisions; more rapid turnover of top personnel in the ranks of the employer, which tends to make the employer less experienced than his union counterpart; and greater sensitivity to public reaction, which may reduce the employer's perceived flexibility in collective bargaining. These factors may contribute to the initial greater acceptance of compulsory arbitration by public employees.

## STATE OF COLLECTIVE BARGAINING

Collective bargaining in the public/nonprofit sector, where it exists at all, is relatively new. While the history of employee organizations in this sector is substantially older, these organizations have been accustomed to spend much of their time in lobbying the legislative bodies that determined wages and working conditions or in "bargaining" with the civil service commissions and personnel departments that administered the various acts. The newness of labor relations for public employees has two effects. First, employees and representative organizations as well as employers are accustomed to a process of wage setting and administration by others. They may have had some influence in determining working conditions but not a final voice. Second, there has been no tradition of collective bargaining and joint setting of conditions. Both the stage of bargaining and the previous process are important. The introduction of compulsory arbitration concomitant with or soon after that of collective bargaining means that the parties' roles and expectations are more flexible. In the case of hospitals, too, the introduction of compulsory arbitration occurred soon after collective bargaining and before bargaining processes and relationships had become established.

## THE SPEED OF THE COMPULSORY ARBITRATION PROCESS

A notable aspect of compulsory arbitration, wherever it has been authorized in the United States, is the speed of the arbitration process. The reason for such speed is not difficult to understand: a slow process in resolving deadlocks would only lead to irritation of feelings and aggravate the conflict. Most states with legislation on compulsory arbitration make sure that the bargaining and resolution of deadlocks will not drag on by specifying a timetable for the entire process. This assures a terminal date for disputes after the start of bargaining. The parties may decide to wave certain dates in the prescribed timetable to accommodate the process to their own circumstances, but such time alterations are mutually agreed on and therefore do not produce irritating delays.

## THE USE OF PRIVATE ARBITRATORS

To facilitate speedy aribtration, compulsory arbitration in the United States is usually within the jurisdiction of private arbitrators. Only Nebraska has chosen to assign disputes and other labor relations matters to a Court of Industrial Relations. The use of private arbitrators means that the parties may have any one of a number of persons as the impartial arbiter in their dispute, with the arbitrator's availability being the only condition of his accepting the case. The arbitrator is usually acceptable to the parties because he is someone who has had considerable experience in arbitrating. Some states increase the degree of acceptability by providing the parties with a panel of third-party arbitrators from which the parties must choose the person to hear their case.

## REACTION TO POSSIBLE
## SUBVERSION OF ARBITRATION

The possibility exists that either party may become dissatisfied with the results of the arbitration and hence with the arbitration process. In that case, actions to show displeasure and to release frustration could subvert compulsory arbitration as a method of resolving disputes. In fact, the dispute would be extended and not ended. Up to this point in time, no serious subversions of this type have occurred. Employers have engaged in legal maneuvers, generally to test the constitutionality of compulsory arbitration and to question particular points in awards. Employees and their representative organizations have also not always been satisfied with particular awards. Both parties realize, however, that compulsory arbitration is not an indelibly fixed component of their bargaining system. Compulsory arbitration has usually been adopted as an expedient; in Michigan, it has frankly been adopted as an experiment. Thus, both parties realize that extreme actions in opposition to compulsory arbitration would end the entire process and place them in a worse position. They have more to lose by not following the process than by swallowing occasional awards that they regard as unfavorable. The possibility of a legislature's withdrawing compulsory arbitration if it proves ineffective appears to act as a deterrent to its being disregarded.

## PUBLIC ACCEPTANCE OF
## COMPULSORY ARBITRATION

Compulsory arbitration has long been regarded as inconsistent with free collective bargaining. Yet the public has accepted arbitration as a reasonable and acceptable way of resolving disputes between employers and employees in certain functions and occupations. Whatever the costs involved in the process and its outcome, the public regards the price as a fair one to pay for an absence of strikes by the affected employees.

The relative importance of these factors to the success of compulsory arbitration may be debatable. Some conditions would seem to be requisite for compulsory arbitration. For instance, the basic *sine qua non* is acceptability of the process by all concerned. Other conditions may not be essential in order for compulsory arbitration to succeed, but they seem to contribute to the willingness of the parties to submit their case to compulsory arbitration and to the ability of the arbitrators to arrive at a conclusion. In any case, these conditions have facilitated the acceptance of the concept of compulsory arbitration to resolve bargaining impasses. The next section will focus on the process of arbitration.

## Structuring Compulsory Arbitration

The possibility of variations in the compulsory arbitration process with subsequent different implications has escaped those who deny the possibility of compulsory arbitration in a collective bargaining system. Even those who favor compulsory arbitration often lack imagination as to possible differences in form. The problem is important, for the structure of compulsory arbitration may determine the extent of its use and its usefulness.

The existing statutes on compulsory arbitration provide a field laboratory for studying some possible differences in the structure of compulsory arbitration and the effects of these differences [10]. One can easily uncover variations in each of the provisions common to arbitration statutes: time devoted to bilateral bargaining before an impasse can be declared, the presence and role of administrative agencies in the impasse procedure, the method of selecting the impartial arbiter, the allocation of arbitration costs, and ability to appeal the procedure or results. Differences in each of these areas will affect the frequency of implementing arbitration, difficulties in the process, and even to some degree satisfaction with the entire idea of compulsory arbitration

Rather than discussing in detail each of the areas just mentioned, we shall concentrate on a few to illustrate the issue of structure. Three possible ways of structuring compulsory arbitration will be considered together with their implications for collective bargaining: limiting the scope of arbitration, providing intervening steps between impasse and arbitration, and imposing costs when arbitration is implemented.

Limiting the subjects that can be submitted to arbitration may also limit the occasions on which disputes terminate in arbitration. The Canadian statute, for instance, has excluded certain topics from arbitration awards:

    a. Provisions requiring legislative implementation;
    b. Awards dealing with "standards, procedures, or process governing the appointment, appraisal, promotion, demotion, transfer, lay off or release of employees, or with any term or condition of employment that was not a subject of negotiation between the parties during the period before the arbitration was requested . . .";
    c. Terms and conditions of employment covering employees outside the bargaining unit for which arbitration was requested [11].

The limitations on arbitrable subjects cannot be so restrictive, of course, as to render arbitration meaningless. Limitations may preserve necessary interests, direct arbitrators in their scope of action, and alert the parties to the narrow, if important, uses of arbitration. Certainly many subjects that cannot be arbitrated are of concern to employees and management and may therefore be negotiated. Excluding such items from arbitration encourages the parties to bargain, if possible, on these items but prevents their settlement by a third party. To this extent, exclusion may in fact encourage bargaining while permitting specific immediate interests to be settled by arbitration, if necessary.

A second structural method to affect the incidence of compulsory arbitration has been to provide steps between the declaration of a bargaining impasse and the onset of arbitration. Half of the U.S. statutes providing for compulsory arbitration require mediation prior to arbitration. Arbitrators operating under other statutes find that often initially they are, in effect, mediators and sometimes are able to settle differences. A controversy has surrounded the interjection of mediation, fact finding, or other types of resolution techniques short of and prior to compulsory arbitration. When the parties know their dispute *may* end up in arbitration, the argument runs, they will be as unwilling to be guided by mediators as they were to negotiate directly. In fact, mediators themselves have felt frustrated at times because they could not compel the parties to accept mediation. Perhaps some sort of mediator's certificate of conformance could be made a prerequisite to compulsory arbitration and would thus encourage unwilling parties to work with the mediators. The fact remains that mediation, wherever and however it is used, has been successful in sharply reducing the number of impasses that are submitted to compulsory arbitration.

A third method, one that has not yet been tried, could involve monetary costs to both parties. A major difference between strikes and compulsory arbitration is that the latter involves relatively few direct costs to the parties. In some states, the allocation of costs permit the employees to escape any cost in compulsory arbitration; even so, the costs to the municipal employer are generally nominal. Only when the size of the employer or the employee group involved is very small may cost considerations provide an effective deterrent to frequent use of compulsory arbitration. Penalizing both parties for using compulsory arbitration could make it more like strike action. It would thus place on both parties the responsibility for and the cost of arbitration. Both sides would have to weigh the cost of bargaining a settlement versus the anticipated benefit of an arbitrated award, less the monetary penalty. The detailed form of the penalty needs to be worked out. Clearly it must be calculated on a per-member and per-citizen basis. Perhaps it can be made variable, depending on the number and types of issues to be resolved. Or it could be left up to the arbitrator to assess the impasse penalty. The proceeds of the penalty could be contributed to charity or to some civic purpose from which neither side could benefit directly. Again, the purpose of such a penalty (or cost of arbitration) is not to prevent arbitration but to encourage bargaining.

Other aspects of the arbitration process could be structured so as to encourage bargaining and reserve arbitration for those cases where a true bargaining impasse exists. The point is to consider alternatives and their effects.

## Conclusion

Terminal procedures to collective bargaining disputes are admittedly a knotty problem. The right to strike is being increasingly challenged as a rational, responsible way of resolving disputes; in some areas, its appropriateness is questionable. A number of alternative measures have been advocated, including compulsory arbitration.

Traditionally, compulsory arbitration and collective bargaining have been held incompatible. Recently these has been a new interest in compulsory arbitration as an effective ingredient in the bargaining process. These two positions may actually be closer to each other than they seem to be initially. Some of those who oppose compulsory arbitration in connection with collective bargaining imply that their arguments are valid only if compulsory arbitration were regularly available as a terminal impasse procedure in all collective bargaining situations. Isaac concedes:

> ... it may be that in the public service and certain public utilities where it may be desirable to avoid political entanglements, state intervention along the lines of a wage board should be made for wage determination and other industrial matters [12].

At the same time, some proponents of compulsory arbitration believe that even if compulsory arbitration is rational and feasible, the climate of labor relations does not permit its implementation as a general answer to labor disputes. Rather, these proponents favor limited initial utilization of compulsory arbitration and revised thinking about possibly extending its use. The important issues, then, may not be whether or not compulsory arbitration should be permitted as an end to labor disputes. Events have outstripped theory and already provide an answer to that question. The evidence to date in Canada and the United States suggest that compulsory arbitration is possible under certain conditions and that the traditional arguments against its use are inapplicable. The problem now is to determine which cases compulsory arbitration may be an appropriate terminal procedure and how compulsory arbitration should be structured in these cases to maximize the viability of collective bargaining. This paper has suggested some answers to these questions.

## REFERENCES

1. See, for instance, the Governor's Committee on Public Employee Relations, State of New York, *Final Report* (March 31, 1966), pp. 15-16, and Herbert R. Northrup, *Compulsory Arbitration and Government Intervention in Labor Disputes* (Washington: Labor Policy Association, Inc., 1966).
2. The following is based on the article by J. E. Isaac, "Compulsory Arbitration in Australia" in *Collective Bargaining: Selected Readings*, edited by Allan Flanders (Penguin Books, 1969), pp. 193-211. The article is an excerpt from "The Prospects for Collective Bargaining in Australia," *The Economic Record*, December 1958, pp. 347-361.
3. Kenneth F. Walker, *Industrial Relations in Australia* (Cambridge: Harvard University Press, 1956), and J. E. Isaac, *Trends in Australian Industrial Relations* (Melbourne: Melbourne University Press, 1962).
4. This section is a summary of Orme W. Phelps, "Compulsory Arbitra-

tion: Some Perspectives," *Industrial and Labor Relations Review*, XVIII (October 1964) pp. 81-91.

5. Cf. Carl M. Stevens, "Is Compulsory Arbitration Compatible with Bargaining?" *Industrial Relations*, V (February 1966), pp. 38-52.

6. J. Douglas Muir, "Canada's Experience with the Right of Public Employees to Strike," *Monthly Labor Review*, XCII (July 1969), pp. 54-59.

7. Robert G. Howlett, "Innovation in Impasse Resolution," paper prepared for New York University, February 11, 1970, pp. 40-43. (Mimeographed.)

8. J. Joseph Loewenberg, "Compulsory Arbitration for Police and Fire Fighters in Pennsylvania," *Industrial and Labor Relations Review*, XXIII (April 1970), pp. 367-379. Also J. Joseph Loewenberg, "Compuslory Binding Arbitration in the Public Sector," paper for International Symposium on Public Employment Labor Relations, New York City, May 4, 1971.

9. For an elaboration of differences between employers in the public and private sectors, see Michael H. Moskow, J. Joseph Loewenberg, and Edward C. Koziara, *Collective Bargaining in Public Employment* (New York: Random House, 1970).

10. Loewenberg, "Compulsory Arbitration."

11. Canada, *Public Service Staff Relations Act of 1967*, LXXII (70).

12. Isaac, "Compulsory Arbitration," p. 205.

*       *       *

Dr. Loewenberg is an Associate Professor in the School of Business Administration of Temple University. He has had extensive experience as a labor economist with the U.S. Department of Labor, and has served as a member of the National Labor Panel, American Arbitration Association, National Center for Dispute Settlement, and the New Jersey Public Employment Relations Board. Prof. Loewenberg has authored numerous articles and texts related to public-sector bargaining.

## Discussion Questions

1. Why has it been said that compulsory arbitration and collective bargaining are inherently incompatible? Give pros and cons.
2. Describe some differences in bargaining motivations between employers in the public and private sectors. How would compulsory arbitration fit into this scheme?
3. Do you believe that inexperience in bargaining techniques might make compulsory arbitration more or less desirable?
4. Discuss the use of public versus private sector-experienced arbitrators in public sector disputes. Is it a good idea to limit public sector arbitration to those experienced in the public sector? Why, or why not?

*Reprinted from Journal of Collective Negotiations in the Public Sector, Spring, 1972*

## CHAPTER 8

# *Mechanisms for Resolving Collective Bargaining Impasses in Public Education**

**DR. HARRY A. BECKER**
*Dean of Graduate Studies*
*Westfield State College*
*Westfield, Massachusetts*

### The Impasse

"There is no point to any further talk. This is an impasse. We're leaving". The speaker was the chief negotiator for the teachers' association. He and his associates picked up their papers and walked away from the bargaining table. The next day, the press carried a statement by the association negotiators accusing the board of education of not bargaining in good faith.

It was indeed an impasse. When either or both parties announce that it is impossible to reach agreement at the bargaining table *and refuse to continue bargaining*, an impasse exists.

An impasse is a crisis. It amounts to an announcement that the process of collective bargaining is not an effective means to reach agreement on whatever the issues are.

In theory, an impasse may be triggered by either party. In practice, the impasse is a tactic of the employee organization. The employer has nothing to

---

* Presented at the American Association of School Administrators Convention, Atlantic City, February 21, 1976.

72

gain from the breakdown of the collective bargaining process. The employer can afford to talk on and on. On the other hand, the employee organization wants and needs an agreement as soon as possible. If it requires an additional month or an additional year to reach agreement, it is likely to mean that wage increases and benefits will be lost for an additional month or an additional year.

An impasse may be the inevitable consequence of endless hours of bargaining without reaching agreement. Day after day, the negotiators began bargaining as the sun was setting and continued through the night until the sun was high in the heavens. But agreement could not be reached on issues believed to be vital. The time arrived when the spokesman for the employee organization announced, "There is no point to any further talk. This is an impasse".

On the other hand, the impasse may be a matter of strategy. The employee negotiators may believe that they have gotten as much as they can through the process of collective bargaining, but that what they got is not enough. They may believe that by creating an impasse, pressure can be applied that will produce additional concessions.

No generalization can be made as to whether an impasse is an unavoidable breakdown in the bargaining process or whether the impasse is a matter of strategy. The fact is that it may be either. A judgement on this matter can be made only by careful analysis on a case-by-case basis.

One has only to review the hundreds of impasses that have occurred in bargaining in the field of education to realize that an impasse can occur whether or not mechanisms are provided for resolving an impasse and reaching a settlement. The impasse is a fact of collective bargaining life. The inevitable conclusion is that if a due process for settling the impasse has not been provided, both legal and illegal actions will take place in the attempt to force a more favorable settlement.

In education, the impasses that have occurred in collective bargaining for a contract have been resolved sooner or later—in one way or another. Illegal methods, including the job action and the strike, have usually, though not always, been effective in winning concessions that had been refused at the bargaining table.

Mechanisms for resolving impasses necessarily utilize the services of third parties. Mediation, fact finding, and arbitration are the major mechanisms. There is no panacea, but there is convincing evidence that third parties can be effective in reaching agreements. Let us analyze the third-party mechanisms most frequently advocated or utilized.

## Mediation

Mediation is the mechanism where a third party tries to negotiate an agreement between the two principal parties. The mediator meets in Kissinger style with each party separately. The mediator's object is to move the two parties closer together, to close the gap between the positions taken at the time that the impasse occurred. The mediator goes back and forth between the two parties. If there is more than one mediator, they may separate and work with both parties simultaneously.

The mediator tries to reason with each party and tries to be persuasive and convincing. He tries to show how the available conditions of agreement are advantageous to whichever party he is working with. If he succeeds in bringing the parties close together, he will have a joint meeting with both parties. At that meeting, if an agreement can be hammered out, the mediation has been successful.

The mediator is trying to find a formula for settlement that both sides will accept. The mediator is not seeking primarily to determine what settlement would be right and fair. The mediator must be pragmatic. Mediation succeeds only when and if both parties are willing to agree. One mediator said, "If both parties will agree that the moon is made of green cheese, that is O.K. with me".

Mediation is usually provided as a conciliation service by a state agency in accordance with state law. In Massachusetts, mediation service is provided by the State Board of Mediation and Arbitration. There is usually little or no choice as to the persons who will mediate or whether there is one mediator or more than one.

Mediators have no authority. They do their best to negotiate a settlement. Mediation succeeds if both parties believe that the available settlement is as good as they can get.

## Fact Finding

Fact finding is a widely used third-party mechanism. Fact finding is also often a service provided by a state agency in accordance with state law.

While mediation tries to negotiate a settlement that each party believes is to its advantage, fact finding tries to appeal to both parties to be reasonable and to be mindful of the welfare of the children and the public interest.

The fact finder will request that all pertinent information be submitted. He will make such investigation as he sees fit. A hearing is held at which both parties and also other persons can present the facts as they see them. The fact finder deliberates and evaluates all of the facts that have been obtained. A fact-finding report is issued. This report includes recommendations for settling the dispute or impasse.

The fact-finding report is public information, but is not binding on the parties. If fact finding succeeds in getting the parties to agree on a settlement, it is because both parties have been convinced that the fact finder's recommendations offer as favorable a settlement as they are likely to get and that the consequences of prolonging the impasse will be unfavorable. If public opinion has been crystallized in support of the fact finder's recommendations, the prospects of a settlement are enhanced.

As can be expected, fact finding does not always succeed in bringing about a settlement. For example, the Colorado Springs teachers overwhelmingly rejected a fact finder's recommendations to settle a dispute on the provisions of the new contract. Two days later, on December 4, 1975, the teachers voted to strike for the first time in the city's hundred-year history. The strike that began on December 4 lasted for twelve days.

## Arbitration

Arbitration is potentially the most valuable third-party mechanism for settling disputes. Arbitration is essentially a judicial proceeding. The arbitrator or arbitrators hold hearings at which each party to the dispute or impasse submits evidence. The arbitrators render a decision that is called an award. This decision is similar to the verdict of the court in a civil lawsuit. The award spells out what action is to be taken with regard to each of the issues in the dispute.

There are two kinds of arbitration: binding arbitration and nonbinding arbitration. Compliance with the award is compulsory in binding arbitration. In nonbinding arbitration, compliance is optional. Each party considers the award and makes a decision as to whether or not to accept it.

In the public school sector, school boards and state legislatures have been wrestling with the problem of what to do about arbitration since the famous Norwalk, Connecticut case in 1951.[1] This case arose as part of the aftermath of the 1946 Norwalk teacher strike, which was one of the first teacher strikes in the United States. Along with the animosity engendered by the strike, the board of education and teachers' association quarreled bitterly about their respective rights and their correct relationships. The teachers' association claimed both the right to negotiate a group contract and to employ arbitration to settle disputes. Legal counsel for the teachers' association encouraged the lawsuit in the belief that the court would mandate binding arbitration as the mechanism to use in settling disputes. In the Norwalk case, the Connecticut Supreme Court of Errors rendered a declaratory judgment that was intended to provide guidelines for the relationships and rights of both the teachers' association and the board of education.

With regard to arbitration, the declaratory judgment of the Connecticut Supreme Court of Errors in the Norwalk case limited the use of arbitration "to certain, specific, arbitrable disputes". The Court declared:

> . . . If it is borne in mind that arbitration is the result of mutual agreement, there is no reason to deny the power of the defendant (the

[1] The author was Superintendent of Schools in Norwalk, 1953-1970.

board of education) to enter voluntarily into a contract to arbitrate a specific dispute. On a proposal for a submission, the defendant would have the opportunity of deciding whether it would arbitrate as to any question within its power. Its power to submit to arbitration would not extend to questions of policy but might extend to questions of liability. Arbitration as a method of settling disputes is growing in importance and, in a proper case, "deserves the enthusiastic support of the courts". . . . Agreements to submit all disputes to arbitration, commonly found in ordinary union contracts, are in a different category. If the defendant entered into a general agreement of that kind, it might find itself committed to surrender the broad discretion and responsibility reposed in it by law. . . .

The best answer we can give . . . is, "Yes, arbitration may be a permissible method as to certain specific, arbitrable disputes".

Twenty-five years later, this decision still prevails with regard to binding arbitration.

## Available Mechanisms are Ineffective

In grievance procedures, it has become common practice to have some type of third-party procedure as the final step. Some grievance procedures even provide for binding arbitration.

We must keep in mind that grievances usually deal with issues of liability. An individual or a group claim that under the contract or established policies they are entitled to some benefit or privilege such as more pay or more time off. The issues are certainly important to the individuals concerned, but in a relative sense, the stakes are small to the board of education.

On the other hand, in negotiating a collective bargaining agreement, the stakes are high. It makes a big difference what new fringe benefits and salary schedules are established. These and other policy decisions can commit very large amounts of money. In the Norwalk case, the Connecticut Supreme Court of Errors declared that under existing Connecticut law, it would not be legal to delegate policy decisions to a third party.

In the twenty-five years since the Norwalk case, the Connecticut legislature has enacted several laws that establish and regulate collective bargaining in public education. There has not been legislation, however, to require or empower Connecticut school boards to use the mechanism of binding arbitration to settle collective bargaining impasses. The situation is similar in most of the other states. Only a few states provide for some form of binding arbitration. Wisconsin, for example, permits binding arbitration, but only if both parties enter into it voluntarily.

What conclusions can be drawn as to the effectiveness of available mechanisms for settling collective bargaining impasses? In most situations, if binding arbitration is available at all, it is available only for grievance actions. The mechanisms available in collective bargaining impasses are just not effective.

Teacher strikes have become more and more common. In the 1969-70 school year, there were 181 teacher strikes. By 1970, an NEA survey reported that three out of four teachers believed that at least in some circumstances, teachers should strike. In the fall of 1975, 170 teacher strikes kept an estimated 2,000,000 children from attending classes. Teacher strikes are occurring in all parts of the country and in school districts of all sizes.

## Impasses and Strikes are Costly for All Concerned

Many teacher associations are ready to accept binding arbitration, but school boards and legislatures are not. Why is this so? Judging from the statements made by those who are opposed to teacher strikes, it is a carry-over from the past when school boards could dictate salaries and working conditions and it was not necessary to reach a bilateral agreement.

A retired teacher who opposes teacher strikes said,

> . . . No one should be permitted to shut down a government operation for which taxes have been levied.
> . . . public employees are a part of government, and strikes by government are intolerable and undemocratic too.
> Strikes by government employees are a step on the road to chaos and anarchy, as well as a defiance of the voters and elected officials [1].

Another educator who opposes teacher strikes declared:

> . . . Teachers who violate the law should be dealt with severely. They should know better. Law-breaking teachers cannot possibly instill in their students a respect for the law. In states with no-strike laws, contracts should include the stipulation that any teacher who violates the law is automatically fired [2].

Some who are opposed to legislation to provide binding arbitration believe that binding arbitration would give teachers greater benefits than they could otherwise obtain. These people prefer a weaker mechanism such as nonbinding arbitration. Nonbinding arbitration can be accepted or rejected by the board of education.

Of course, this is true. What these people overlook is that nonbinding arbitration can also be accepted or rejected by the teacher association. Under present conditions, it is actually possible for the teacher association to reject the nonbinding arbitration award, go on strike, and obtain a settlement that is greater than the arbitration award.

This is just what happened in Norwalk, Connecticut in 1969. Contract negotiations were stalemated and an impasse was declared. After mediation efforts failed, the dispute was submitted to nonbinding arbitration. At issue were wage and fringe benefits with an estimated cost of approximately $400,000.

The arbitrators' award provided wage and fringe benefits with an estimated cost of $100,000. The Board of Education voted to accept the arbitrators' award, but the Teachers' Association rejected the nonbinding award and voted to strike. An injunction forbidding the strike was ineffective. After a four-day strike, the board of education and the teachers' association reached a settlement with wage and fringe benefits having an estimated cost of $300,000. This settlement was duly ratified by the Norwalk Common Council.

Had there been binding arbitration, the settlement would have been in accordance with the arbitrators' award. The cost to the city would have been approximately $200,000 less. Even more important, everyone would have been spared the turmoil, disruption, and animosity engendered by a strike.

Tom James, Associate Director of Communication, Education Commission of the States, reached the conclusion that "the record of state action promises that teacher power has little chance of becoming the ogre that many people expect" [3]. The alarmists are unrealistic because it is contrary to the "public will".

## Teachers Are No Longer Docile

Times have changed. Increasingly, teachers are unwilling to accept wages and conditions that they believe to be unsatisfactory. Terrel H. Bell, U.S. Commissioner of Education, recalled how it used to be:

> . . . Each year, we simply drew up a new salary schedule and presented it to the teachers as a gift from the benevolent father. And the teachers, hat in hand, said, "Thank you" [4].

As Paul Friggens wrote, this is no longer true [4]. Ronald Corwin said that what seems to be new about teaching "is the scope and intensity of teacher militancy" [5].

Public school teachers are determined to have an active role in the decision-making process. To achieve this they are well organized. When they believe it is necessary, teachers will violate antistrike laws.

The dissatisfaction and disillusionment of many teachers with present collective bargaining legislation is expressed by one teacher in the following:

> . . . The collective bargaining law does not work as it is now written. School committees still hold all the cards and can sit back and say No, No and No.
>
> This year we have exhausted what is available to us in bargaining in Massachusetts law. . . .
>
> What other alternative is left for the teachers to receive an equitable settlement—a strike, which is illegal.

Until the "collective begging" law is changed and teachers are given the right to strike, I am afraid there will be more and more teacher unrest, slowdown, sickouts and strikes. . . . [6].

The thousands of teachers who are willing to strike are not ordinary criminals. Many of them strike reluctantly and with the conviction that there is no alternative. As one teacher expressed it:

. . . As a teacher and current member of a negotiating team, I fully support the right of public employees, including teachers, to strike. The decision, however, is an extremely painful and personal one for the individual involved. Often this decision takes place in agonizing circumstances because there is no other way out. . . .

Teachers who have exhausted the legal remedies available (labor boards, mediation, fact finding, etc.) and are still faced with no possibility of settlement after long, weary months of attempting to be reasonable may be left with only two choices: strike or crawl back on their knees. In such a case, there is really only one choice to make. If legislators, school boards, et al. deplore strikes, then it behooves them to provide strong alternatives through which public employees may seek redress for unresolved disputes. . . . [7].

Here is a teacher who prefers binding arbitration. Under present legislation, however, the strike is the only available action that is effective. This is how he expressed his views:

. . . Strikes are disruptive, costly, and technically illegal; they are also effective when all else fails. Without them we are reduced to humbly petitioning the elected school officials for whatever they are disposed to offer us—take it or leave it.

A system of binding arbitration would be a major improvement and an acceptable substitute, but until a fair, workable plan is offered, we're stuck with the strike. . . .

The strike is unwieldy and it hurts to use it, but it works and it's all we've got. The fact of its being illegal is unfair but has to be disregarded until a viable alternative presents itself. We may not yet have the right to strike, but we certainly have a moral and a professional obligation to be willing to strike when no other recourse is available [8].

More and more people believe that under existing circumstances, teacher strikes are justifiable. The widespread sympathy for striking teachers is illustrated in the New Haven teacher strike in the fall of 1975. The judge jailed ninety teachers for violation of a no-strike injunction. A thousand non-teaching school employees staged a sympathy walkout over the jailing of the teachers. Labor leaders, angry over the judge's refusal to release the ninety jailed striking teachers, called a one-day citywide walkout by 30,000 union workers. The walkout was approved by all 146 leaders of the ninety-two unions comprising the Greater New Haven Central Labor Council. The

President of the Greater New Haven Central Labor Council called the jailings "a miscarriage of justice. These people are not criminals. They are not law-breakers, no matter what the Judge says" [9].

## Court Imposed Penalties Are Ineffective

Penalties imposed by the courts are not effective deterrents to teacher strikes. When teacher strikers are sent to jail, they receive admiration, sympathy, and increased support.

In the New Bedford, Massachusetts strike, twenty-seven teachers were jailed and the teacher association had to pay a fine of more than $337,000 by June 1, 1976. As a result, teachers associations throughout Massachusetts have launched a campaign to support the New Bedford Teachers by contributions to pay the fine. As has been noted, in the New Haven strike, jailing ninety teachers only produced a sympathy walkout by 30,000 union workers.

Fining and jailing teacher strikers have been counterproductive. Such judicial sanctions have increased the bitterness and determination of the strikers.

## No Reprisal Provisions

Striking teachers have learned to insist on so-called "no reprisal" or "amnesty" clauses in a settlement. The purpose of these clauses is to prevent the board of education and administration from punishing or discriminating against the strikers.

Colorado Springs suffered a twelve-day strike in December, 1975. The teachers rejected a settlement solely because it contained insufficient amnesty provisions for the 1,200 strikers. When the amnesty provisions were improved, the Colorado Springs Teachers Association (CSTA) accepted the settlement. The amnesty provisions obtained by the Colorado Springs strikers include:

1. striking teachers return to the same positions they occupied prior to the strike;
2. there will be no board retaliation against members of the CSTA negotiations unit, nor any teacher who participated in the walkout;
3. there will be no retaliation against CSTA members for picket activities;
4. there will be no strike-related entries made in teachers' personnel files;
5. teachers close to retirement who participated in the strike retain full-service credit [10].

## Teacher Strikes Have Been Legalized in Three States

In three states, Hawaii, Oregon, and Pennsylvania, teacher strikes are permitted under these conditions:

The strike is being called by the exclusive bargaining agent;

All impasse procedures have been exhausted;

A specified number of days has elapsed since the fact-finding board made its recommendations public;

The exclusive bargaining agent has given notice of its intent to strike;

The employer has had an opportunity to petition the public employee relations board or a court of law in the event of danger to the public's health and safety [11].

## What Legislation is Needed?

There is no doubt that legislation is needed, but there is confusion as to what that legislation should provide. What is needed is legislation that will provide an effective mechanism for resolving collective bargaining impasses in an equitable manner. Binding arbitration as the final step for resolving impasses is an effective mechanism. Possibly, it is not the only effective mechanism.

Legalizing strikes in public education, however, does not provide an effective due process for settling impasses. The strike is an extreme form of protest. Legal or not, there have been hundreds of strikes in public education every year. Unless an effective mechanism is provided, there are likely to be hundreds of teacher strikes in the years ahead. Legalizing teacher strikes does not solve the problem. For all concerned—teachers, children, taxpayers—the strike is a disruptive, disturbing, wasteful, and expensive action. Moreover, strike action does not necessarily lead to the equitable settlement of an impasse. The solution that is forged in the heat of a strike may be based on pressure and emotion. Moreover, the animosity that thrives in a strike and the recrimination that follows it, provide a poor climate for harmony and cooperation in the day-to-day administration of whatever settlement is made.

What is needed is a wise legislative solution rather than the legislative endorsement of an extreme form of protest. After twenty-five years and more than a thousand teacher strikes, there should be no doubt that there is urgent need for an effective mechanism. In the spirit of Thomas Edison, "There is a better way and we have found it". Legislation should be enacted to provide binding arbitration as the final step in settling collective bargaining impasses. It is time for the responsible, sensible people in all communities to call for constructive, effective legislation.

## REFERENCES

1. H. Nixon, of Melrose, Massachusetts, in letter printed in *NEA Reporter, 15,* p. 3, February, 1976.
2. B. McMahon, Reading Consultant in Ridgefield, Connecticut Public Schools, in letter printed in *The Common, 4,* p. 4, February, 1976.

3. T. James, The States Struggle to Define Scope of Teacher Bargaining, *Phi Delta Kappan, 57,* p. 97, October, 1975.
4. Quoted in P. Friggens, Teachers on the March, *Reader's Digest,* p. 112, February, 1976.
5. R. G. Corwin, The New Teaching Profession, *Teacher Education,* 74th yearbook of the National Society for the Study of Education, Chap. IX, p. 231, 1975.
6. F. Knox, Vice President, Medford, Massachusetts Teacher Association, in letter printed in *The Common, 4,* p. 4, December, 1975.
7. K. Trudell of Burlington, Vermont, in letter printed in *The Common, 4,* p. 4, February, 1975.
8. C. J. Barton, Quinsigamond Community College, Worcester, Massachusetts, in letter printed in *The Common, 4,* p. 4, December, 1975.
9. Quoted in *Boston Sunday Globe,* November 23, 1975.
10. *NEA Reporter, 15,* p. 13, February, 1976.
11. K. H. Ostrander, Collective Bargaining Laws in Education, *National Association of Secondary School Principals Bulletin, 59,* p. 21, September, 1975.

\*                    \*                    \*

Harry Becker is Dean of Graduate Studies and Continuing Education at Westfield State College. He previously served as Superintendent of Schools at Norwalk, Connecticut for seventeen years. Dr. Becker is also the past president of the Connecticut Association of Public School Superintendents and Director of New England Association of Public School Superintendents.

Dr. Becker has authored numerous articles on collective bargaining, and has served as a consultant to local districts and state boards from coast to coast.

## Discussion Questions

1. Discuss the advantages and disadvantages of each of the impasse resolution methods described.
2. The author states that mediation is usually provided as a conciliation service by a state agency. Why would this be so? What is the state's interest in conciliation?
3. Why is binding arbitration used more frequently for resolving grievances than for settling bargaining impasses? Discuss the question from a legal, moral, and pragmatic point-of-view.

*Reprinted from Journal of Collective Negotiations in the Public Sector, Vol. 5(4), 1976*

# PART II
# RESOLVING STRIKES

Strikes in the public sector present a particularly thorny problem, in that the services being withheld are often essential to the well-being of the community. Police, firefighters, sanitation workers, public hospital personnel—their right to strike is plainly at odds with the public's right to protection and care.

The usual solutions to this problem involve arbitration or the courts, but in the article included here J. H. Foegen presents an innovative approach. He suggests letting the taxpayers decide—before a strike—whether certain controversial issues should be granted or not. Both the governmental employer and the union would have to agree beforehand to accept the taxpayers' decision. Would this prevent strikes? Read and consider.

The following articles in this section deal with strike situations—on the premise that strikes are often viewed as a failure by the parties to conclude a contract and as the ultimate act of frustration. This view is a natural reaction stemming from the fact that in nearly all states, strikes are prohibited. In the private sector, where strikes are permissable, the strike is just another mechanism in the arsenal of tools available to bring about a settlement.

Perhaps if we in the public sector were to put aside the question of legalities, we would view the strike weapon as another objective technique that can be used to resolve an impasse. The three articles after the strike prevention paper deal with consequences and causes—the first with quasi-strikes, the second with the sociology of a strike, and the last with the effect of bargaining laws on the public employee's tendency to strike. All of these papers show that strikes may be considered as a point along the continuum from bargaining through conciliation efforts to the final contract.

# CHAPTER 9

# *Public Sector Strike-Prevention: Let the Taxpayer Decide*

**J. H. FOEGEN, PH.D.**
*Professor of Business*
*Winona State University*
*Winona, Minnesota*

When parties to a labor dispute cannot agree on a new contract, the ultimate settlement resort is the strike. Where private sector nonessentials are concerned, such "wars of attrition" are relatively tolerable. But union growth and militancy today is in the public sector, where strike-caused interruptions of vital services can be more serious. Legislatures are granting the legal right to strike, and where they have not yet done so, workers have struck illegally.

But all agree that this is not the best way to settle disputes, regardless of apparent short-run gains. A taxpayer referendum might be better than either a strike or conventional arbitration as a way to prevent public-sector walkouts.

When bargaining stalemates involve government employees, some form of arbitration has been the best strike alternative yet proposed. It is one way to get the help of supposedly objective third parties, along with mediation, conciliation, fact finding, and labor courts.

It is often seen as the most effective of these methods. Mediation and conciliation lack arbitration's finality; the "outsider" cannot actually decide the issue. While completely rational, and potentially helpful, fact finding can be mere delay; and it does not necessarily produce a decision either. Labor courts would ease the burden on the regular judicial system and would tap labor expertise, but nothing substantial has yet come of this method in the United States. (Among other reasons, labor people remember how courts have dealt with unions in the past.)

Not only can arbitration be effective, but it is already familiar through its widely accepted use as the final step in grievance procedures. Adopted voluntarily to make industrial relations systems work more smoothly, it is often called "*administration* arbitration." The contract has been signed; the arbitrator's role is only to interpret its meaning, or to fill unanticipated gaps until the next negotiating sessions.

Strike-avoiding arbitration, though related conceptually, is much less accepted. In fact, in a rare show of agreement, both unions and managements have opposed such "*negotiation* arbitration." In this case, the contract is still being written; the arbitrator, in settling a dispute, is helping to write the contract. Having done his job, he customarily moves on, leaving the parties to live with his decision. Though desiring strike-avoiding settlements, both parties have resisted such reliance on "outsiders." They have not even approved voluntary negotiation arbitration, much less the compulsory kind.

As a lesser evil, however, voluntary negotiation arbitration may be a technique whose time has come. One researcher [1] reported that "both management and unions are more open-minded toward the use of contract arbitration than is generally supposed." Supporting a greater likelihood of use, he noted such things as a "growing intolerance of strikes," and the impression that "unions are no longer considered by many people to represent the . . . underdog." Furthermore, "the conventional view that collective bargaining cannot exist without the right to strike is being subjected to increasing examination." In his opinion, urgent national problems requiring large public expenditures, which in turn require continued economic growth, do not allow national administrations of whatever party to idly watch strikes that affect many and that could contain collectively the seeds of recession.

As a major current example of this less adamant posture, the steel industry's Experimental Negotiating Agreement[1] can be cited. Intended to prevent a national strike when the industry's contract came up for renewal in 1974, it was approved by the Steelworkers Union's Basic Steel Industry Conference on March 29, 1973, and

---

[1] The agreement permits strikes on a local level.

signed shortly afterwards by representatives of ten major companies.

"On the national level, both sides will start talks no later than February 1, 1974. If an agreement is not reached by April 15, either party can submit their (sic) unresolved bargaining issues to an Impartial Arbitration Panel, which will have authority to render a final and binding decision on such issues. This arbitration panel will be made up of one Union representative, one representative of the companies, and three impartial arbitrators selected by both sides. At least two of these three arbitrators to be chosen by both sides will be persons thoroughly familiar with collective bargaining agreements in the Steel Industry. This panel will hear any disputes during the month of May, 1974, and must render its decisions no later than July 10, 1974. The balance of July will be available for the implementation of the Panel's award. The renewal date for the Basic Steel Agreement is August 1, 1974" [2].

Despite nice-sounding language and good intentions, however, even the steel industry admits that the adoption of this agreement embodying voluntary negotiation arbitration is "experimental." Theoretically, the dislike for having an outsider write the contract will provide incentive for avoiding stalemates that could go to arbitration. But since the parties themselves write the rules, and abidance is voluntary, its viability remains to be tested.

In the meantime, the problem in public employment is more urgent than in the steel industry. While steel is basic to the economy, garbage pickup and police and fire protection are even more so. Service interruptions can pose serious difficulties even in school operations and in the U.S. Postal Service, not to mention the volunteer Army.

Fortunately, a rare kind of arbitration uniquely suited to the public sector might be a solution. The slate of labor-management relations in government employment is still relatively clean; rules are still being developed. Resistance to negotiation arbitration in the public sector, therefore, could be overcome easier than in private industry.

The proposal is this: assuming both sides want to settle the dispute fairly and without a strike if possible, they might be convinced to keep working under the old contract until the next election. The critical issues should be on the ballot as a taxpayer referendum. And the union and the employing agency must be persuaded to agree in advance to abide by the voters' decision [3]. For example, one likely issue might be posed on the ballot this way: "Do you approve granting a wage increase of "X" cents per hour to our police officers, at an estimated additional annual cost to property taxpayers of "Y" mills?" Convincing the parties to go this route could be accomplished, among other ways, by newspaper editorials, pressure by the League of Women Voters or other groups, or persuasion by a mediator.

If voters approve, the union would get what it wanted, and the taxpayers who would pay the bill would have no cause for complaint.

If the proposal is rejected, the union has agreed in advance to abide by the decision and not to strike. This would actually happen for a number of reasons:

1. The union's integrity would be at stake; is it as good as its publicly-given word or isn't it?
2. The rejection would be by a majority of voters, rather than by a few "biased" bargainers;
3. "Social responsibility" is an increasingly important concept. Corporations have been prodded into accepting it in many ways; profit-maximizing is said to be no longer enough. Colleges are being pressured into "accountability" for their use of tax money; "if it's education, it must be good" is less accepted than before. Unions have not felt the impact as much, but action here is past due, and they are a likely next target;
4. The issues can be re-submitted to the voters if desired, since elections occur fairly often.

As always with innovative proposals, objections can be expected. For instance, it will be said that all voters are not property taxpayers. While true, most are, at least indirectly via parents or landlords. That is sufficient. Nor are all municipal services financed entirely through property taxes. Some state funds are used, thus making all voters eligible.

It will also be argued that all union members would vote approval of wage and benefit increases en bloc, in support of the "universal brotherhood of organized labor." But this is highly debatable. Bloc delivery of the "labor vote" on other matters has been questioned increasingly as all voters have shown more independence. At the very least, union members' tradeoff between their pocketbooks and their feelings of solidarity toward members of other unions is still not totally clear. Even the directly involved, public employee union member has a dual role: as a tax-paying citizen, and as a tax-receiving public employee.

The argument that referenda are awkward can be countered by noting that they are nevertheless not uncommon. Furthermore, the use suggested here would be infrequent. Only in stalemated vital situations would they be used; if private-sector experience is any guide, most negotiations will be settled amicably; referenda will not be needed.

Finally, in a far-from-exhaustive list, a powerful objection can be made that taxpayers would never agree to raise their own taxes; by definition, this requires compulsion. But school bond issues are approved. Reasonable capital improvements, as well as rising expenditures made necessary by urban expansion and inflation are agreed to indirectly via actions of elected officials. And since the collective fairness of voters can be assumed, they would very likely be sympathetic to well-justified employee demands. As an extreme example, if city employees had gone years without raises, if the cost of living had been rising continuously, and if other local unions had been getting increases, the outcome of a referendum would be predictable.

In short, there is a growing need to find a fair, nonstrike way to settle stalemated public employee disputes that involve necessary services. Just because they work for government, people cannot reasonably be expected to settle for second-class economic citizenship; they have a right to "look out for number one" the same as anyone. But denial of vital public needs for private gain is also a questionable practice.

Since arbitration has long been accepted as a workable solution in grievance procedures, since resistance to voluntary negotiation arbitration seems to be abating, and since a better practical alternative is not yet available, letting the taxpaying voters act as a collective arbitrator via referenda is worth considering.

## REFERENCES

1. Jack Steiber, Voluntary arbitration of contract terms, Bureau of National Affairs *Daily Labor Report*, 85: 18-19, May 1, 1970.
2. I. W. Abel, "ENA . . . A Better Way," 1973. Pamphlet No. PR-217 is available free from: United Steelworkers of America, Five Gateway Center, Pittsburgh 15222.
3. For other views on this idea, see the independently developed article by Sam Zagoria, "Referendum Use in Labor Impasses Proposed," in the *Proceedings of the 25th annual meeting of the Industrial Relations Research Association*, Madison, Wisc., 1972. Also, the *Monthly Labor Review*, May, 1973.

*       *       *

Dr. Foegen is currently a Professor of Business at Winona State University. He has published 64 articles to date in various professional journals. He is a member of the Industrial Relations Research Association, the American Society for Personnel Administration, and the International Personnel Management Association.

# Discussion Questions

1. In the public sector, when an arbitrator helps settle a strike by making a decision that the taxpayers must accept, does this constitute an usurpation of the power delegated to elected officials?
2. If the taxpayers were to vote on contract clauses and conditions, would this help or hinder the negotiations process? Why? How?
3. What recourse would employees have in an area where taxpayers continued to vote down pay raises, legitimate or not?

*Reprinted from Journal of Collective Negotiations in the Public Sector, Summer, 1974*

# CHAPTER 10

## *Quasi-Strikes by Public Employees*

**DR. PAUL D. STAUDOHAR**
*Associate Professor of*
*Business Administration*
*California State University, Hayward*

Despite recent legislation in Vermont, Hawaii, Pennsylvania, Alaska, Minnesota, and Oregon, the legal right to strike continues to be withheld from public employees in most jurisdictions. It appears that many state legislatures are awaiting the outcome of experiments that grant a limited right to strike before they move toward liberalization on this sensitive issue. Meanwhile, illegal strikes continue to occur throughout the nation. When confronted with the task of applying a statute or interpreting the common law in cases of a public employee strike, judges have almost invariably determined that the right does not exist unless specifically granted by statute.

An interesting feature of litigation over public employee job action is a group of cases in which a plausible argument can be made that the action taken by the employees cannot be considered strike action within the meaning of a no-strike statute or in light of the common law. When public employees engage in such "quasi-strikes," they try to express dissatisfaction with government decision making or policies, exert pressure to have their demands accepted, and/or call their grievances to the public's attention, without running afoul of the law. Such job action is calculated to bring pressure by withholding all or a portion of labor service, similar to that of a strike, but contemplates circumvention of the law by use of tactics not strictly barred by legal mandate. Public employees have also attempted to distinguish strike activity, quasi and conventional, on the grounds that they are exercising constitutionally protected rights.

## Strike Criteria

Strikes by public employees are made illegal by statute, court decision, and attorney general's opinion. A starting point in determining the legality of quasi-strikes is to examine statutory proscriptions, if any, in a jurisdiction. Statutory definitions of strikes range from narrow to comprehensive. New York's Taylor Act simply defines strike as " . . . any strike or other concerted stoppage of work or slowdown by public employees." [1] Hawaii's more extensive description notes that:

"Strike" means a public employee's refusal, in concerted action with others, to report for duty, or his wilful absence from his position, or his stoppage of work, or his abstinence in whole or in part from the full, faithful, and proper performance of the duties of employment, for the purpose of inducing, influencing, or coercing a change in the conditions, compensation, rights, privileges, or obligations of public employment; provided, that nothing herein shall limit or impair the right of any public employee to express or communicate a complaint or opinion on any matter related to the conditions of employment. [2]

In these and other strike definitions can be found certain criteria that job action must have in order to be considered a strike under a strict interpretation of the law. If the job action in question does not possess those criteria that the law's strike definition encompasses, it may escape any prohibitions against strikes that the law includes. Five criteria were found: 1) the employees in question are public employees; 2) there is an employer-employee relationship; 3) there is a refusal to perform all or a part of the job duties of the employees; 4) job action involves employees acting in concert; and 5) the purpose of the job action is to pressure for more favorable terms. The following circumstances and law cases illustrate the application of criteria to quasi-strike activity.

## Tactics Employed and Application of Criteria

Slowdowns and speedups are not only difficult to prosecute under anti-strike laws, but also offer certain economic advantages to the employees that other pressure tactics do not. Slowdowns occur when workers pay extra careful attention to the rulebook. The effect on output can be dramatic, as when correction officers in New York City in 1972 cut the number of inmates sent to court to 28 from a normal 600. [3] Speedups, where police in a "ticket blitz" give two or three times the normal number of citations, can generate substantial publicity, and pressure from an irate citizenry. Refusal to work and concerted action criteria make slowdowns and speedups of questionable illegality. As a federal court noted, "We stress that it is only an actual refusal by particular employees to provide services that is forbidden (by the laws). [4] Other advantages are that workers can continue to collect their pay because they have not stopped work as in a conventional strike, dues payments to the employee organization continue, and strike benefits do not have to be paid.

One of the most frequently used quasi-strike devices is the sickout. Public employees have "caught" red rash, blu flu, Russian diarrhea, and various other arcane maladies. It is hard to prove intention to engage in concerted activity when large numbers of employees call in sick. A court might reason that the act of an unusual mass of employees afflicted is presumption of concerted activity, and that it is incumbent on the individual employee to prove illness. However, ease in obtaining a spurious doctor's certificate may thwart this approach. Air traffic controllers who conducted a sickout in 1970 were found by federal courts to be engaging in the legal equivalent of strikes. [5] A similar rationale has been used at the state and local levels in allowing court orders against this activity. Proportion of the work force taking action will vary and can determine whether the employer seeks to have the action officially declared a strike. Disruptions that involve withholding services of all or a large portion of the work force in a sickout are more likely to result in a request for a court order than job actions in which a small portion of the work force calls in and where normal duties and work load are carried out. Yet, once court action is sought and the issue of the legal right to strike is joined, it may not matter that service was carried out at normal levels. In a case that did not involve a sickout but that illustrates the point, firefighters claimed they were engaged in a "work dispute," and not a strike when fire stations were manned by 50 per cent of normal staff and there was no adverse effect on service. The Appellate Court of Illinois determined that "The fact that the work stoppage was not complete does not alter the obvious purpose of the firemen to realize their demands by withholding their services." [6]

Mass resignations, while a potential device for circumventing no-strike laws, have in at least two decisions been declared illegal. In one case, public school teachers claimed they were not employees at the time of their mass resignations during summer vacation since they had not yet signed new contracts after the expiration of their old ones. The Supreme Court of Michigan found that the employment relationship continued, lack of a contract notwithstanding. [7] In a similar case involving teachers, the New York Supreme Court said, "Defendants, in contending that a strike is not the same as the so-called resignations, are urging a distinction without a difference; the argument is specious and sham and is rejected." [8] However, in another mass resignation case a restraining order obtained by a school board recognized the teachers' right to effect lawful resignations. [9]

Mass leaves of absence were used as a tactic in a Minnesota job action. Following a work stoppage, teachers claimed to be exercising their rights to a leave of absence for purposes other than conducting a strike. Reasons given by the teachers' association as justifying leaves of absence during the strike were: the impossibility of teaching because of unruly students; the fear of personal harm if picket lines were crossed; the avoidance of confrontation with professional colleagues who were on the picket line, and additionally, to call attention to the problems of public education. The Minnesota Supreme Court decided that the teachers who requested leaves of absence during the strike were entitled to a hearing on whether they were in violation of the state's no-strike law. [10]

In litigation applying anti-strike law, a question may arise as to what employees are classified as "public." Employees of an agricultural improvement and power district, which was a political subdivision of the state of Arizona, went on strike to enforce execution of a collective bargaining agreement. A key distinction behind the Supreme Court of Arizona's permitting the strike was that the district was owned by private landowners and its employees were paid from private funds. [11]

A related issue is whether public employees engaged in a

proprietary function, [12] as opposed to a governmental function, can be excluded from a strike prohibition. The distinction involves the question of whether the government entity is acting with the primary objective of seeking to further its own corporate ends or as a servant of the state in a particular capacity. Courts have rejected this distinction, standing alone, on at least two occasions. [13]

A distinction that has been accepted by courts involves situations in which employees are given the right of collective bargaining and the right to engage in concerted activities by statutory language close to that employed in the National Labor Relations Act. In one case, transit authority legislation gave collective bargaining and concerted action [14] rights to employees who had previously had these rights prior to public takeover. The right to strike was not expressly granted in the legislation. An important fact leading to the California Supreme Court's decision to allow the strike was that the transit authority had taken over two private transit companies whose employees had the right to strike, and the transit authority legislation provided that if a privately owned public utility was taken over, the employees were not to incur any worsening of benefits as a result of the acquisition. [15] In a more recent California case a similar issue came before the state's Court of Appeal. In the transit authority legislation in question, the right of collective bargaining was given, but no mention was made of rights to engage in concerted activities as there had been in the earlier case. The court nevertheless determined that the collective bargaining rights granted in the legislation contemplate and imply a right to strike. The court also distinguished the proprietary activity of the transit workers from other public employees when it stated that "(W)e deal only with government operation of a normally private, proprietary activity ... our holding in no way extends to 'public employees such as policemen, firemen and public officers exercising a portion of the state's sovereign powers.' " [16] This case may have implications for transit district employees in other jurisdictions.

## Constitutional Issues

Public employee strikes, quasi and conventional, raise certain constitutional issues that, it can be argued, prevent application of the strike ban. Even though there may be a matching of characteristics of the job action with criteria under the law, constitutional rights may be deemed denied by application of the law to a particular case. The constitutional rights most likely to be brought up are free speech, right of assembly, and right to petition government for redress of grievances—granted by the First Amendment of the U.S. Constitution to U.S. citizens, and extended to persons in their capacity as citizens of the states by the Fourteenth Amendment; due process of law—Fifth Amendment, as extended by the Fourteenth Amendment; prohibition of involuntary servitude—Thirteenth Amendment; and equal protection of the laws—Fourteenth Amendment.

Denial of First Amendment rights may be charged by employees where there is an absolute prohibition on strike activity in the law. Apart from the prohibition itself, it may also be alleged that language used to outlaw any participation in a strike at any time is vague and overly broad, and causes employees to fail to exercise other protected First Amendment rights because of fear of overstepping the line. On neither the statutory strike prohibition *per se* nor language used therein have courts ruled that constitutional rights of speech, assembly, or presentation of grievances were violated. [4] However, a requirement that federal employees sign an affidavit pledging not to advocate strikes, or to become a member of an employee organization that does, was struck down by a federal district court as violating the First Amendment. [17]

In response to claims of violation of constitutional rights of due process of law, courts have noted that there is no absolute right to strike under the Constitution and that the right to strike cannot be considered a fundamental right that would come under protection of the due process clause. [18] An interesting application of due process occurred in a case involving Florida teachers who engaged in a statewide work stoppage in 1968 by submitting mass resignations. The teachers were reinstated and given back tenure status, but were required to pay $100 as a condition for reemployment with tenure. The teachers argued that the forced extraction of the payment for reemployment was a penalty for an undefined legislative wrong, in violation of their rights of due process, since they were given no hearing or opportunity to protest the payments. The U.S. Court of Appeals held that the teachers had no rights of reemployment because of their resignations. The teachers were offered an opportunity to give the $100 in return for reinstatement, and the court felt that this kind of mutually advantageous exchange could not be considered a deprivation of property. [9]

Involuntary servitude, prohibited by the Thirteenth Amendment, has been charged in seeking to permit public employee strikes. The principal argument is that by not allowing employees the legal opportunity to strike, or in the face of an injunction against a threatened or ongoing strike, the person is ordered to work against his will. The position courts have taken in response to these allegations is that because the employee has the option and is free to resign at any time, performance of personal service against the will of the employee is not compelled. [19]

Violation of equal protection rights of the Fourteenth Amendment has been alleged on the grounds that private employees have the right to strike by law while public employees do not, and that the distinction between the two types of employees in the law is arbitrary, irrational, and invalid. The charge might also be brought if some public employees in a jurisdiction are given the right to strike while others, such as police and fire fighters, are not. Courts have not been receptive to these claims, as exemplified by the U.S. District Court's statement that:

> (I)t is not irrational or arbitrary for the Government to condition employment on a promise not to withhold labor collectively, and to prohibit strikes by those in public employment, whether because of the prerogatives of the sovereign, some sense of higher obligation associated with public service, to assure the continuing functioning of the Government without interruption, to protect public health and safety or for other reasons. Although plaintiff argues that the provisions in question are unconstitutionally broad in covering all Government employees regardless of the type or importance of the work they do, we hold that it makes no difference whether the jobs performed by certain public employees are regarded as "essential" or "non-essential," or whether similar jobs are performed by workers in private industry who have the right to strike protected by statute. Nor is it relevant that some positions in private industry are arguably more affected with a public interest than are some positions in the Government service. [20]

## Summary

This research indicates that quasi-strikes present an opportunity for avoiding the ban on public employee strikes. However, they may be found to violate the law. The rationale used by courts in considering quasi-strike activity to be statutorily unlawful is that the legislative purpose or spirit is effectuated by holding related job action, apparently designed to accomplish the same result as a strike, to be within the purview of the statutory proscription.

Courts have generally been unresponsive to claims that a ban on public employee strikes violates constitutional rights. Lack of an absolute right to strike makes what might otherwise be applicable First Amendment and due process protections mostly inoperative. Freedom to resign employment has been held by courts to negate involuntary servitude contentions. Court rulings have consistently found no denial of equal protection of the laws by favoring private employees with a strike right.

## REFERENCES

1. New York Ch. 392, L. 1967, as amended, Sec. 201(9).
2. Hawaii Revised Statutes, 1970, Ch. 89, Sec. 2(17).
3. *Wall Street Journal*, October 26, 1972, p. 1.
4. *United Federation of Postal Clerks v. Blount*, 325 F. Supp. 879 (1971). Affirmed on appeal, 404 U.S. 802 (1971).
5. *Government Employee Relations Report*, No. 333, January 26, 1970, p. B-11.
6. *City of Rockford v. Local No. 413, International Association of Firefighters*, 240 N.E. 2d 705 (1968).
7. *School District for the City of Holland, Ottawa and Allegan Counties v. Holland Education Association*, 157 N.W. 2d 206 (1968).
8. *Board of Education of City of New York v. Shanker et al*, 283 N.Y.S. 2d 548 (1967).
9. *National Education Association, Inc. et al v. Lee County Board of Public Instruction et al*, 69 LC 12,999 (1972).
10. *Head v. Special School Dist. No. 1*, 208 N.W. 2d 294 (1973).
11. *Local 266, International Brotherhood of Electrical Workers, AFL v. Salt River Project Agricultural Improvement and Power District*, 275 P. 2d 393 (1954).
12. For example, working for a municipal corporation set up to provide water, transit service, or garbage collection.
13. See: *Port of Seattle v. International Longshoremen's and Warehousemen's Union*, 324 P. 2d 1099 (1958); and *South Atlantic & Gulf Coast District of International Longshoremen's Association, Independent, et al v. Harris County-Houston Ship Channel Navigation District*, 358 S.W. 2d 658 (1962).
14. Specific language was "to engage in other concerted activities for the purpose of collective bargaining or other mutual aid or protection."
15. *Los Angeles Metropolitan Transit Authority v. Brotherhood of Railway Trainmen et al*, 355 P. 2d 905 (1960).
16. *Alameda-Contra Costa County Transit District v. Amalgamated Transit Union, Div. 192, et al*, cited in full in *California Public Employee Relations*, No. 16, March, 1973, p. 57.
17. *National Assoiacation of Letter Carriers v. Blount*, 305 F. Supp. 546 (1969). The decision was not appealed.

18. *City of New York v. DeLury*, 295 N.Y.S. 2d 901 (1968); and *Adkins v. Myers*, 239 N.E. 2d 239 (1968).
19. *In re Block*, 236 A. 2d 589 (1967); *Pinellas County Classroom Teachers Association v. Board of Public Instruction of Pinellas County*, 214 So. 2d 34 (1968); and *Jefferson County Teachers Association et al v. Board of Education of Jefferson County, Kentucky*, 75 LRRM 2486 (1970).
20. *United Federation of Postal Clerks v. Blount*, op. cit., p. 883. See also, *City of New York v. DeLury*, op. cit., and *School Committee of the Town of Westerly v. Westerly Teachers Association*, 82 LRRM 2567 (1973).

## Discussion Questions

1. Discuss some of the consequences for employers, employees, taxpayers, and governments of withholding the right to strike from public employees.
2. Consider the moral aspects of speed-ups and slow-downs among essential service employees. Who is affected, and how?
3. Discuss the First Amendment as it applies to the right to strike and its converse—denial of the right to strike.

*Reprinted from the Journal of Collective Negotiations in the Public Sector, Fall, 1974*

# CHAPTER 11

# Public Employee Bargaining Laws and the Propensity to Strike: Case of the Public School Teachers

**ROBERT J. THORNTON**
*Assistant Professor of Economics*
*Lehigh University*

**ANDREW R. WEINTRAUB**
*Assistant Professor of Economics*
*Temple University*

Over the past decade, perhaps no issue in the subject of labor relations has evoked quite as much controversy as the public employee strike. Moreover, among public employees there has been no group nearly as militant in its bargaining tactics as public school teachers. Prior to 1965, usually only a handful of teacher strikes occurred in any given year. Since that time, however, the number of teacher strikes has literally mushroomed until presently more than one hundred such strikes are witnessed annually across the United States. (See Table 1.) Moreover, strikes by public school teachers generally comprise from 25 to 30 per cent of all public employee strikes each year.

Concurrent with this upsurge of strikes there has also been

Table 1.  Teachers' Strikes in the United States, 1946-1972

| Year | Number of Teachers' Strikes | Year | Number of Teachers' Strikes |
|---|---|---|---|
| 1946 | 14 | 1960 | 3 |
| 1947 | 20 | 1961 | 1 |
| 1948 | 10 | 1962 | 1 |
| 1949 | 5 | 1963 | 2 |
| 1950 | 0 | 1964 | 9 |
| 1951 | 6 | 1965 | 5 |
| 1952 | 7 | 1966 | 30 |
| 1953 | 1 | 1967 | 98 |
| 1954 | 2 | 1968 | 85 |
| 1955 | 1 | 1969 | 118 |
| 1956 | 5 | 1970 | 148 |
| 1957 | 2 | 1971 | 126 |
| 1958 | 0 | 1972 (through June) | 20 |
| 1959 | 2 | | |

Sources: Department of Labor, U.S. Bureau of Labor Statistics and Research Division, National Education Association.

observed a steady growth in the number of state laws granting collective bargaining rights to public school teachers (and to other groups of government employees as well). Although only three states had enacted such laws prior to 1965 (Alaska, New Hampshire, and Wisconsin), there are presently twenty-seven state statutes that permit at least some form of collective bargaining for public school teachers.

These statutes vary greatly in form, however. For example, some states mandate that the school board *bargain* collectively with the union or association representing the teachers (e.g., Michigan). Other states simply require that the board "meet and confer" with the teacher representatives (e.g., Oregon). In still other states, school boards are authorized, but not required, to negotiate with teacher representatives and may sign agreements that may or may not be binding on the two parties. Nevertheless, despite the many substantive differences, until recently these statutes remained in agreement with respect to one essential feature: their unanimous refusal to condone the use of the strike weapon by teachers. In 1970, this unanimity was broken when two states—Pennsylvania and Hawaii—passed laws that permitted the use of the strike by teachers and certain other government employees in instances where the public health or safety was not involved [1].

## The Influence of Legislation

The fact that the number of teacher strikes has risen nearly *pari passu* with the number of state bargaining statutes over the past decade has led to some interesting speculation. Principally, has the passage of legislation permitting teachers to bargain collectively been directly responsible for the rise in the propensity of teachers to strike despite the fact that such legislation generally declared the strike to be illegal? This concern was first expressed more than six years ago by Robert Doherty and Walter Oberer following the rash of teacher strikes in the state of Michigan: "The Michigan experience suggests that the express statutory recognition of the right of teachers to bargain collectively carries with it the likelihood of increased strike activity, even though the latter be declared illegal [2]."

It seems reasonable that bargaining legislation would increase the *propensity* of teachers to strike, even though a state's legislation governing the collective bargaining rights of public school teachers does not include the *right* to strike. One of the basic prerequisites for the successful execution of a strike is a viable organization. Most collective bargaining statutes governing school teachers set up machinery that provides for the recognition of the union and the organization of its collective bargaining activity. Since the strike has always been the ultimate weapon in a union's bargaining strategy, it seems unrealistic to assume that it will be completely disregarded because its use is illegal, especially since the costs of striking seem to be low. Because the penalties provided by the laws against strikes are often so harsh, there is good reason to suppose that they will not be enforced. (How can a school board, for example, fire and replace 20,000 striking teachers?)

Moreover, there has been ample historical documentation of the influence of legislation on strike activity in general. Following the passage of the Wagner Act in 1935, which substituted legal machinery for other organizing and recognitional techniques, the aggregate number of strikes fell sharply, primarily because the change in the legal environment eliminated some important reasons for striking. A similar result followed the passage of the "anti-union" Taft-Hartley Act in 1947, after which the number of strikes fell sharply [3]. Finally, the passage of the Landrum-Griffin Act in 1959 seems to have triggered an increase in strike activity, probably due to the fact that it encouraged dissident groups within unions to make leaders more sensitive to rank-amd-file demands [4].

On the other hand, persuasive as the arguments above may be, the close temporal correlation between teachers' strikes and state bargaining legislation may be illusory. Indeed, the cause-effect relationship may be exactly the reverse of that postulated above, the legislation being largely a *result* of the outbreak of teacher's strikes. Certainly a major reason behind the passage of many state laws permitting collective bargaining for teachers was that a major cause of strikes—viz., recognition—would be eliminated. In fact, a similar development does seem to have presented itself in the late 1940's when the first rash of teacher strikes occurred. Several states followed suit with repressive legislation, legislation that granted no bargaining rights for public employees but instead imposed a set of harsh sanctions on strikers.[1]

This alternative contention is not without the support of many observers of collective bargaining in public employment. According to John Burton and Charles Krider, who have just completed an in-depth examination of the determinants of strikes by state and local noneducational governmental employees: "Those states which encourage collective bargaining because they believe this is a meritorious way to determine working conditions do *not* incur a rash of strikes as a result [5]." Other observers claim further that many more strikes could be avoided by affording all public employees collective bargaining rights [6].

### The Evidence

It is the contention of the present authors that much light can be shed on the controversy regarding the influence of legislation on teachers' strikes by comparing the strike records of the various states on a disaggregated basis. In Table 2, such a comparison has been made for the 27 states with teacher bargaining legislation in effect through 1972.

In all, 646 teachers' strikes occurred in the United States public elementary and secondary schools from July 1960 through June 1972. Of these 646 strikes, 390 of them (or more than 60%) occurred in states *pursuant to* the passage of collective bargaining legislation encompassing teachers.

Columns 3 and 4 of Table 2 show yearly average number of teachers' strikes that occurred in each of the states before and after the advent of permissive bargaining legislation. Excluding the three states for which prelegislation strike data was not available (due to the fact that their bargaining laws were passed prior to 1960), it is to

---

[1] New York's Condon-Wadlin Act of 1947, for example, was considered a model for antistrike legislation during the post-World War II period. The act provided for reemployment of workers involved in strikes but banned pay increases for three years following the strike.

Table 2. Teachers' Strikes in States with Permissive Bargaining Legislation for Teachers, 1960-1972[a]

| State and Effective Date of Earliest Bargaining Statute | Number of Teachers' Strikes 1960-72 | Annual Average Number of Teachers' Strikes | | Number of Teachers' Strikes—12 Months | |
|---|---|---|---|---|---|
| | | Preceding legislation | Following legislation | Preceding legislation[b] | Following legislation |
| Alaska (1959) | 1 | N.A. | 0.1 | N.A. | N.A. |
| California (12/65) | 32 | 0.2 | 4.8 | 0 | 1 |
| Connecticut (6/18/65) | 28 | 0.0 | 4.0 | 0 | 0 |
| Delaware (10/31/69) | 0 | 0.0 | 0.0 | 0.0 | 0.0 |
| Hawaii (7/1/70) | 0 | 0.0 | 0.0 | 0 | 0 |
| Idaho (7/1/71) | 1 | 0.1 | 0.0 | 0 | 0 |
| Kansas (3/23/70) | 0 | 0.0 | 0.0 | 0 | 0 |
| Maine (9/30/69) | 0 | 0.0 | 0.0 | 0 | 0 |
| Maryland (6/15/68) | 9 | 0.4 | 1.5 | 2 | 3 |
| Massachusetts (7/12/66) | 11 | 0.0 | 1.9 | 0 | 2 |
| Michigan (7/23/65) | 162 | 0.2 | 23.6 | 1 | 9 |
| Minnesota (5/23/67) | 1 | 0.0 | 0.2 | 0 | 0 |
| Montana (7/1/71) | 2 | 0.2 | 0.0 | 0 | 0 |
| Nebraska (10/23/67) | 0 | 0.0 | 0.0 | 0 | 0 |
| Nevada (4/28/69) | 2 | 0.2 | 0.0 | 2 | 0 |
| New Hampshire (1955) | 4 | N.A. | 0.3 | N.A. | N.A. |
| New Jersey (4/1/69) | 48 | 2.5 | 7.9 | 8 | 10 |
| New York (9/1/67) | 46 | 0.9 | 8.2 | 3 | 5 |
| North Dakota (7/1/69) | 1 | 0.1 | 0.0 | 1 | 0 |
| Oklahoma (9/9/71) | 5 | 0.1 | 0.0 | 0 | 0 |
| Oregon (8/13/65) | 0 | 0.0 | 0.0 | 0 | 0 |
| Pennsylvania (10/21/70) | 110 | 4.2 | 41.1 | 7 | 58 |
| Rhode Island (5/11/66) | 10 | 0.3 | 1.3 | 0 | 0 |
| South Dakota (7/1/69) | 1 | 0.1 | 0.0 | 1 | 0 |
| Vermont (9/1/69) | 0 | 0.0 | 0.0 | 0 | 0 |
| Washington (6/10/65) | 2 | 0.0 | 0.3 | 0 | 0 |
| Wisconsin (1959) | 10 | N.A. | 0.8 | N.A. | N.A. |

[a] From Research Division, National Education Association, includes teachers' strike data from July 1960 through June 1972.
[b] N.A. = data not available.

be noted that in only 6 of the 24 states did the annual strike average decline following the enactment of legislation. In all of the remaining 18 states, the average number of strikes per annum either increased (11 states) or remained at a zero level (7 states). In some states the increase in the strike frequency was quite dramatic, such as in Michigan and Pennsylvania.

Columns 5 and 6 of Table 2 emphasize even more strongly the tendency for the number of strikes to inch upwards subsequent to the passage of legislation. Again ignoring the three states with unavailable data, in only 3 of the 24 states did strike activity decline during the 12 months following the enactment of bargaining legislation vis-á-vis the 12 months preceding such legislation. Of the remaining states, the number of strikes increased in 7 states and remained at the same level (zero) in 14.

In brief, from the analysis presented above it must be concluded that the passage of collective bargaining legislation for teachers does not seem to have reduced the propensity of teachers to strike. On the contrary, there appears to be a tendency—though not a universal tendency—for strike activity to increase following the enactment of such legislation.

Several additional points should be made to qualify this conclusion. First of all, it has been pointed out elsewhere that in those states in which government employees are required to recognize and to bargain with unions legally representing a majority of their employees, strikes to *establish* the bargaining relationship have been virtually eliminated [7]. There is every reason to suppose that this tendency also holds true for the case of teachers specifically, though apparently the decline in this type of strike has not been sufficient to offset the rise in the number of strikes concerning other substantive aspects of the bargaining process.

We should also make clear that we do not profess that bargaining legislation is the only determinant of teachers' strikes. About 40 per cent of all teacher strikes in the past 12 years have occurred in states where no such legislation existed. Economic factors, such as the rate of change of prices, are also certainly instrumental in the decision of any group to undertake strike activity [8].

Finally, we do not claim that our data supports the contention that the link between legislation and strikes necessarily holds true for *other* (noneducation) groups of public employees. In fact, preliminary evidence by Burton and Krider [9] suggests that no such link exists. Why such a relationship should exist for the case of teachers and not for other governmental employees is a mystery that we are at a loss to explain.

Nevertheless, our analysis does suggest that as more and more states adopt legislation that sets up collective bargaining machinery for school teachers, the number of teachers' strikes will increase. This conclusion runs counter to the suggestion of other observers that such legislation, by creating an atmosphere that allows teachers to vent their grievances and demands across the bargaining table, will actually reduce the number of strikes among school teachers. Our alternative findings suggest that the granting of collective bargaining rights to teachers increases the probability that strikes will occur, since the strike is historically the strongest weapon in any collective bargaining situation.

## REFERENCES

1. Joel Seidman, State legislation on collective bargaining by public employees, *Labor Law Journal*, pp. 13-22, January, 1971.
2. Robert E. Doherty and Walter E. Oberer, *Teachers, School Boards and Collective Bargaining: A Changing of the Guard*, p. 103, Cornell University Press, Ithaca, 1967.
3. Albert Rees, Industrial conflict and business fluctuations, *Journal of Political Economy*, p. 376, October, 1952.
4. Orley Ashenfelter and George Johnson, Bargaining theory, trade unions, and industrial strike activity, *American Economic Review*, p. 47, March, 1969.
5. John Burton and Charles Krider, "The Incidence of Strikes in Public Employment," paper presented at the Conference on Labor in Nonprofit Industry and Government, Princeton University, May 8, 1973.
6. Edward B. Krinsky, Avoiding public employee strikes—Lessons from recent strike activity, *Labor Law Journal*, p. 472, August, 1970.
7. John Burton and Charles Krider, The role and consequences of strikes by public employees, *Yale Law Journal*, p. 438, January, 1970.
8. For an analysis of the economic determinants of strike activity see Robert Thornton and Andrew Weintraub, "The Determinants of Teachers' Strikes: 1946-1970," paper presented at the 1973 Meetings of the Pennsylvania Conference of Economists.
9. Burton and Krider, p. 40.

*         *         *

Dr. Robert J. Thornton is assistant professor of economics at Lehigh University, having formerly been employed as a research assistant for the Brookings Institution. He has published several articles concerning collective negotiations for public school teachers which have appeared in a number of professional journals.

Dr. Andrew Weintraub is currently assistant professor of economics at Temple University. His published research includes articles in numerous professional journals. He is also editor of the volume, *The Economic Growth Controversy,* which is published by the International Arts and Science Press.

## Discussion Questions

1. Discuss how the formal granting of bargaining rights might lead to more or less strike activity than before the legislation was enacted.
2. What factors might lead to a public union's decision to strike?
3. Discuss the "theory of rising expectations" as it might apply to public employees being granted bargaining rights. What are some logical outcomes?

*Reprinted from Journal of Collective Negotiations in the Public Sector, Winter, 1974*

# PART III
# RESOLVING GRIEVANCES

The articles in this section deal with the resolution of impasses that arise after the fact, so to speak. These impasses—for that is truly what they are—occur as a result of problems that stem from administration of the negotiated contract. In effect, the resolution of negotiations impasses may lead directly to the creation of grievances, which need, in turn, to be resolved.

The way this happens deserves some attention. One reason for grievances lies in the contract language. In reaching the original negotiated agreement, the parties compromised or were forced to compromise. The compromises are then written in contract language acceptable to both parties, but since the parties never *really* agreed on the items in the first place, the contract language used is apt to be vague, ambiguous, and/or misleading. Furthermore, the persons who negotiate the agreement are often not the same persons who draw up the final wording of the contract—that is often left to lawyers. Thus, there arises the distinct possibility of a "slip twixt the cup and the lip." Grievances arise because employees interpret what the contract says in one way, while management interprets it another way. The grievance process must determine what the writers of the agreement *really* meant to agree upon. Grievance resolution is, therefore, a nearly inevitable consequence of impasse resolution.

In this section, the authors describe grievance resolution techniques such as arbitration. The president of the American Arbitration Association (AAA), Robert Coulson, leads off by discussing the use of arbitration in settling grievances,

He describes the process from the point of view of the arbitrator and the AAA. In "Arbitrating a Grievance," Hogan gives some practical advice for the parties to a grievance: how and when to file, what to do to prepare for the arbitrator, and who pays. Included is a section on the canons of contract clause construction that tells readers how contract language can lead to grievances. Some court decisions that have had an effect on grievance resolution in education are reviewed by Decker. Kershen's article describes a study that found grievance arbitration decisions to be related to the arbitrator, leading to the question in his title: "How Impartial is Impartial Arbitration when It Involves Public School Teachers?" The final paper in this section tells of the Canadian approach to grievance resolution. The article is especially interesting in pointing up the similarities and differences in attitude and method between the Canadians and ourselves. The most striking such difference, perhaps, is one of scope: federal government employees in Canada are covered by a single federal law, whereas in the United States federal workers are covered under various executive orders that may be changed by successive presidents.

# CHAPTER 12

# The Public Employee and Arbitration

**ROBERT COULSON**
*President*
*American Arbitration Association*
*New York, N. Y.*

A dramatic change is occurring as municipalities, counties, states, and the federal government face up to the fact that their own employees are demanding the right to join unions and to engage in collective bargaining. Something new. Most of this activity has occurred during the past ten years.

Only a quarter of American public employees presently are represented by unions. But the growth of the unions representing such workers has been spectacular, far outstripping the membership gains of labor organizations in the private sector. Teachers, police, fireman, sanitation workers, and virtually every other category of government employes are participating in this movement.

Laws are being passed to accommodate to this trend and, as would be expected under our federal system, each law reflects a unique compromise between various conflicting legislative priorities.

On the one hand, these laws reflect an increasing willingness to recognize the public employee's right to participate in a labor organization. If a majority of the employees in a bargaining unit select a union to represent them, the employer and the union are expected to bargain in good faith toward reaching an agreement over wages and working conditions.

On the other hand, almost all of these laws seek to protect the public against work stoppages, particularly those which would imperil public health or safety. A variety of devices have been utilized to prohibit, or strongly discourage, strikes by public employees.

## Is There a Cure for the Strike?

Traditionally, the right to strike has been prohibited in the public sector by statute and by court decision. In some cases, the penalties imposed have been so harsh that public officials have preferred not to enforce them. Various fines have been assessed against unions and their leaders. Sometimes, jail sentences have been imposed upon union officials, or upon individual strikers. In other cases, court orders have forced the strikers back to work. Not always; sometimes such orders have been ineffectual or have resulted in illegal slowdowns or sickouts. Epidemics of "blue flu" have kept policemen off the streets for several weeks.

Not every strike by government workers creates public inconvenience, much less affects the safety or health of the community. Teachers and other government employees have sometimes discovered that the public can make other arrangements, that their service is not at all "critical." In some parts of the country, there is an increasing willingness to take a strike. There, local government bargains hard, and effectively.

The more enlightened view of American legislators has been to permit a limited right to strike in situations where the public health and safety are not imperiled, but to require both parties to engage in collective bargaining, supported by a variety of third-party services, including mediation, fact-finding and voluntary arbitration. Where a high degree of public risk is involved, compulsory arbitration combined with effective prohibition of the strike is sometimes deemed appropriate.

In some of the larger communities, independent boards have been created to assist in the bargaining. For example, in New York City, the tripartite Office of Collective Bargaining (OCB) has been armed with a variety of procedures calculated to help resolve bargaining impasses: mediation, fact-finding with or without recommendations, a public hearing, advisory arbitration, a cooling-off period, and court sanctions. Recently, OCB was also given the ultimate power of compulsory arbitration. The intent of all of the above procedures has been to provide incentives for participatory self-determination through collective bargaining.

At the same time, collective bargaining needs strengthening. The current emphasis upon unionization and collective bargaining has been reducing public employees' reliance upon the Civil Service system and upon political pressure to obtain employment relief. A recent conference of labor experts, held under the auspices of the American Assembly, concluded that legislative bodies should stay out of collective bargaining. Comprehensive legislation to delineate the scope of bargaining and to ensure its use was strongly recommended. If the trend toward collective bargaining continues, the alternative, traditional systems of regulating labor relations may be expected to diminish. But until they do, such conflicts will create multitudes of grievances and bargaining problems.

## What is the Impact of Collective Bargaining?

Wage settlements imposed upon local governments have created new fiscal problems. In some jurisdictions, the local property tax is no longer able to bear the total burden of providing adequate services. Local governments are begging for additional taxing powers and for state and Federal support. One of the immediate results of collective bargaining in the public sector has been increased pressure upon the helter-skelter structure of local government in the United States. If weaker communities must provide adequate public services, they will demand additional support from other sources of operating tax revenue. As local services increasingly are supported by the more centralized governments, greater pressures may be exerted toward uniformity. In general, the courts are aware of the inequities involved in the present system and will be exerting an influence toward a more even distribution of government services. These considerations will put additional pressure upon the collective bargaining mechanism, reinforcing the trend toward larger bargaining units and more coordinated bargaining by management.

In many urban centers, a substantial portion of public employees come from minority groups. Nevertheless, artificial, non-job-related barriers have existed, creating "white islands" in particular communities, departments, or job classifications. This pattern is now at odds with the well-established national policy toward equal employment, regardless of race, sex, religion, or place of national origin. Since public employers and public unions are dependent on tax revenues derived from the entire population, they are faced with pressure for eliminating barriers in employment. Affirmative compliance programs are being developed. In some cases, implementation of such policies may conflict with job seniority, jurisdiction, or other terms in various collective bargaining agreements. In those situations, it becomes necessary for the public employer and the public union representatives to adjust the traditional structure to permit entry and promotion of minority workers. Various government agencies are engaged in the difficult task of forcing the parties to take whatever steps are necessary to adjust the racial balance of workers and to guarantee equal rights for women.

For all of the above reasons and because the bargaining relationship is still untested, grievances and dislocation will flourish in public employment bargaining units. How will these grievances be resolved?

### Wide-Spread Use of Grievance Arbitration

In the private sector, grievance arbitration has been almost uniformly accepted as the method of choice for resolving the parties' disputes during the terms of collective bargaining contracts. The American Arbitration Association (AAA) participates in such arbitrations as an impartial administrative agency. This very same process is being widely adopted in the public sector. Public cases are heard and determined by the same arbitrators who are used in the private sector. In an increasing percentage of cases, the parties are referring to the Voluntary Labor Arbitration Rules of the American Arbitration Association.

Arbitration procedures in the public sector are of many kinds. Almost any system of arbitration can be administered for the parties by the American Arbitration Association. The AAA rules are designed to give effect to the preference of the parties involved. At the same time, the rules provide a remedy for deadlocks over procedure.

Most public sector parties use *ad hoc* arbitration for the final step of their grievance procedure. They select an arbitrator for each case, without any commitment to use that arbitrator again if another dispute should arise.

From time to time, voluntary arbitration is also used to settle all or some of the issues that parties cannot agree to in collective bargaining. Here the selection of the arbitrator or arbitrators can be particularly important. Again, the AAA can suggest lists of arbitrators or help the parties draft an appropriate submission to arbitration.

Virtually every experienced labor arbitrator is on the AAA panel. AAA Regional Directors keep an up-to-date account of every panel member's experience, availability for quick service, billing practices, and record of acceptability with particular employers and unions. This knowledge is applied when lists are sent to parties in pending cases. AAA lists include the names of arbitrators most likely to be accepted. Thoughtfully composed lists shorten the interval between the filing of a case and the scheduling of a hearing.

In cases administered by AAA, parties usually are able to select an arbitrator by mutual choice from the first list. Where they cannot do so, and where it appears appropriate, second lists are submitted to the parties. Only rarely, when it appears that no agreement is possible, does the AAA make an administrative appointment. In this respect, as in others, the AAA carries out the wishes of the parties when they agree, but provides a way out when deadlocks occur.

The parties can raise procedural matters through the AAA, without having to do so at the hearing. The arbitration hearing is not an ideal place to discuss such matters because each side is then concentrating on making the best possible impression and neither side feels comfortable about suggesting limitations on the scope of the arbitrator's service. For instance, when the parties want to suggest that the written opinion be eliminated, this information can be communicated to the arbitrator by the AAA, without any indication as to which party took the initiative. This can be particularly important to the small public sector union or government union.

## Administrative Procedures

When a case is filed with the AAA, it is assigned to a tribunal administrator, who examines the arbitration agreement to make certain that all procedures required by that agreement are observed. The administrator consults with the parties on special problems or on the need for expedited service, in case of a threatened work stoppage or where a back pay obligation may be mounting. Even in routine cases, this relieves the parties of administrative details. The administrator arranges a convenient date for the hearing and notifies the parties. The administrator also handles requests for a postponement, exchanges of letters, documents and briefs, or requests for a subpoena in advance of the hearing. This practice of communicating only through the tribunal administrator enhances the feeling of confidence each party must have that the arbitrator will not have discussed any aspect of the case privately with the other party. The AAA's role also benefits the arbitrator, for it makes it easier to maintain the standards of conduct the arbitrator is pledged to uphold.

At the hearing, the parties are in a poor position to insist upon a speedy decision. Here, too, the agency role is useful. Under AAA rules, an award must be rendered within the time limits of the parties' contract, or within thirty days after the close of the hearings. As the agent of the parties, the AAA can insist on prompt awards. The AAA must obtain the consent of the parties when extensions of time are necessary. AAA administration helps reduce delay. An AAA case is more likely to be given prompt attention by the arbitrator than one in which no pressure for speed is exerted. A labor arbitrator who consistently fails to meet reasonable time limits may be removed from the active list until such time as he is again able to fulfill his obligations to the parties under AAA rules.

The decision on the substantive issue in dispute is, of course, the arbitrator's. Nevertheless, AAA administration does have an influence on the arbitrator's performance. Before an award is released, the AAA makes certain that the arbitrator has dealt with each issue and has not gone beyond the limits of the submission.

The arbitrator's bill is reviewed at the close of the case. When bills seem too high, they are questioned. Similarly, complaints by a party about the bill or about any other aspect of the case are investigated. The parties have more freedom to voice complaints when dealing through an impartial agency than when the arbitration is not administered. Again, this can be particularly important in the public sector.

Not every public employer and union requires the full range of Association services. Some invoke their arbitration clauses infrequently. But when they do, they sometimes prefer to deal with a private agency rather than another governmental entity. Many parties regard the judgment exercised in composing lists and the greater control of costs as compelling reasons for using AAA services. Other parties occasionally need a tribunal administrator at hearings. There are also situations where, because of an atmosphere of contention, disputes over procedure interfere with the settlement of substantive issues. Here, too, the parties find it to their advantage to leave all technical and administrative decisions to AAA. And finally, there are many who believe that arbitrators observe the limits of their office more closely in supervised tribunals, and this justifies AAA participation, above everything else.

Occasionally, parties discover that their grievance and arbitration system is not functioning as well as they had hoped. They may then wish to turn to the AAA for assistance in redesigning the system or its administration. AAA representatives serve as experienced consultants in such situations.

Staff members of AAA's National Center for Dispute Settlement (NCDS) are particularly well-informed in public sector matters. NCDS was created to offer mediation and other impartial services for disputes involving public employees. Located in Washington, D.C., the NCDS is available for consultation in these matters.

The Association's education department plays a special role in improving the use of labor arbitration. Best results in arbitration are obtained by parties who are well-informed in the use of the procedure. The AAA encourages parties to take a positive approach and sponsors many seminars and training programs for labor and management representatives.

The AAA's programs for training new arbitrators are particularly relevant. The number of active labor arbitrators has not increased in proportion to the demands for their service. The AAA is in a unique position to perform the needed service of training new arbitrators because of its knowledge of the needs of the parties and because it is the only nongovernmental organization in the United States devoted to promoting the use of arbitration.

The American Arbitration Association, at 140 West 51st Street, New York, New York 10020, is a national center for information on labor dispute settlement, both in the private and the public sectors. It publishes three monthly summaries of labor arbitration awards, two of which deal with the public sector: *Labor Arbitration in Government*, which brings together reports of grievance and impasse arbitration decisions in local, state and Federal government employment, and *Arbitration in the Schools*, which specializes in grievances and impasses in the public schools. Further facts and published material are available upon request.

*          *          *

Robert Coulson is President of the American Arbitration Association and a member of the New York and Massachusetts Bar. He has written and lectured extensively on the settlement of disputes. He is Chairman of the Social Policy Committee of the Federation of Protestant Welfare Agencies of New York and also a Vice President and Chairman of the Executive Committee of the Police Athletic League in New York City.

## Discussion Questions

1. What are some of the similarities and differences between grievance arbitration methods and practices in the public and private sectors?
2. Consider the role of the American Arbitration Association in the resolution of grievances. What functions does it serve, and what functions might it serve?
3. Evaluate the present methods of paying for arbitration. What changes might be made to improve these methods?

*Reprinted from Journal of Collective Negotiations in the Public Sector, Winter, 1973*

# CHAPTER 13

# *Arbitrating*
# *a*
# *Grievance*

**JOHN B. HOGAN**
*Member, New York State Bar*

Almost all collective bargaining agreements contain a grievance procedure, yet most public employers have no apprehension of the havoc such a clause can produce. It is a sleeping monster, which can be aroused by your employees snapping their collective fingers. In this article I will describe some of the pitfalls and how to avoid them.

In order to focus attention on preparations for arbitration, this article will be limited to the final step of grievance, whereby the dispute is to be settled by a third party, generally referred to as an arbitrator. Further, I will only discuss an agreement that limits the definition of a grievance to a complaint which involves the interruption of, application of, or compliance with, the provisions of the labor contract. If a labor agreement has a broader definition of a grievance, it will produce additional problems that will not be covered here. An unnecessarily broad definition can open everything including the granting of tenure to a determination by an outside third party. Such arrangements are contractual suicide. Reference will be made to various provisions of New York State Law, the phrase "CPLR" meaning the Civil Practice Law and Rules of New York State. In other states, specific reference should be made to the laws pertaining to arbitration.

Let us assume that a grievance has been processed through the various intermediate steps. Both parties are adamant. What happens now?

First of all, the employee or union files for arbitration of the grievance. When such a request has been made, management must take several important steps.

1. *Review of the notice to arbitrate.* Is it in proper form? The labor agreement should contain the required form of a demand for arbitration. If the agreement refers to the rules of the American Arbitration Association (AAA), the notice of intention to arbitrate (demand) must contain a statement setting forth the nature of the dispute and the remedies sought. A determination that the notice is defective raises the issue of whether a motion should be made in court to stay the arbitration (CPLR 7503). On first impression, it would seem that such a procedure is unnecessarily technical and will accomplish little. But, if the demand is broad, you will be faced with a "shotgun" approach at the arbitration hearing, which will make it impossible to prepare and will confuse the issues rather than clarify them. In such a case, a motion to stay could be considered advisable.

2. *Jurisdiction.* Is there an allegation of the violation of the agreement, and has the grievance been processed in the manner required by the agreement, within the time limits specified by the grievance clause? If an answer to any of these is no, then the application is defective and a stay of the arbitration should be considered (CPLR 7503).

3. *Should the grievance be contested?* The entire issue presented by the demand to arbitrate the grievance should be reviewed again, especially with the employer's attorney. If there is a good chance that the charging party will prevail, now is the time to settle this matter. Possibly, a compromise can be worked out that would save face for each side.

4. *Submission of an answer.* In some grievance clauses an

answer admitting or denying the issues raised in the demand for arbitration is necessary. If such an answer is not served, the allegations may be deemed admitted. In the AAA Rules, if no answer is submitted, all issues are deemed denied. In many cases an answer is advisable. It gives the arbitrator, at an early stage of the proceeding, an idea of the issues and could possibly shorten the proceedings.

5. *Investigation.* There must be a complete investigation of the grievance. It is possible that several of the issues can be admitted. If this is the case, it usually is advisable to do so in order to put greater focus upon the items in dispute. Possibly, parties who might have been reluctant to step forward, during the intermediate steps of the grievance, might now supply information, or give thoughts which might be helpful in the pursuit of the defense of this matter. No one can properly participate in an arbitration hearing unless he has knowledge of all issues, is prepared for the hearing, has gathered all evidence available to rebut the anticipated allegations, and is ready to present intelligently the employer's position.

6. *Representation by the proper party.* In many instances, a trial attorney is not at home in the informal atmosphere of an arbitration hearing. Certainly someone should be present to represent the employer's interest at the proceeding. Until someone on the employer's staff has been through a few arbitrations, a labor attorney, experienced in labor arbitration proceedings in the private sector would be an appropriate choice. Keep in mind that this area is a specialized field, and not every attorney can be expected to be able to fully and adequately represent your interests. When someone on staff has participated in a few grievances, he can handle the average grievance without outside help.

7. *Understanding the language of the proceeding.* Just as you would prepare to visit a foreign land by getting some general idea of its language, you should acquaint yourself with various phrases that are generally used in grievance proceedings. A few of these phrases are:

   a. *Burden of proof*—the party initiating the grievance has the burden of proof. This includes both the burden of producing evidence and the burden of persuasion. The party charged with the burden of proof must produce evidence in order to avoid the risk of an adverse verdict after he has completed presenting his evidence. If insufficient evidence is produced in the first instance, many times the other party will not be required to present rebuttal evidence. Further, the evidence produced must be, in quantity and quality, sufficient to persuade the trier of facts.

b. *Ambiguity*—most grievances revolve around each party's contention that the language of a disputed clause has a meaning most favorable to his respective position. Accordingly, the clause is ambiguous. At least one party, and sometimes both parties will make such a contention. Latent ambiguities are those which become apparent when the contract is applied, while patent ambiguities are those which appear on the face of the instrument, and arise from the defective, obscure, or insensible language used.

Obviously, most disputes pertain to latent ambiguities. In many instances, the arbitrator will give substantial weight to past practice.

c. *Past practice*—is a practice or usage which has been of such long, continued duration as to be of common knowledge to the parties to the contract and is mutually accepted and concurred in by the contracting parties.

At this stage let's try out a few of these phrases. At a hearing the party presented the *demand*, contending that management had violated the terms of the agreement in a certain specified way. The *demand* refers to the particular clause, and presents a factual situation that occurred whereby the clause was not applied in the manner contended by the union to be correct. Management interprets the clause a different way, contending that it would be a violation of the agreement if management acted in the manner which the union contends is appropriate. Both parties are pointing to the same clause to substantiate their contentions. Hence an *ambiguity*. The union contends that the clause, although reasonable on its face, is a *patent ambiguity*, since it was never intended by the parties that the result complained of would occur. Management disagrees and asserts that if the contention of the union is sustained, it would be contrary to *past practice*, which was not demanded to be changed at the bargaining table, although the union had ample opportunity to do so. Management contends that the union has failed in its *burden of proof*, so the grievance should be dismissed.

It is a rare grievance that does not involve

    d. *Canons of Construction.* Many cases are decided by the application of one or more of these principles in relation to the disputed clause in the agreement. Cases are prepared and arguments centered around the Canons of Construction. A few of these are as follows:

        1) Language of the contract is controlling in the absence of ambiguity or fundamental mistakes.

        2) In interpreting contracts, the ordinary meaning of the terms is looked to initially.

        3) Failure of one party to specify what it later claims was intended cannot alter the contract.

        4) A contract clause, if it is clear and unambiguous, will be interpreted in strict accordance with the contract terms, in the absence of positive evidence indicating a contrary intent; implications may not be read into a contract, for the agreement language controls.

        5) Contract terms must be accorded their first and customary meaning, unless it has been past practice and custom of the parties to give a special meaning to the same terms.

        6) A written contract is presumed to be final; failure to include a term is proof that it was intended to be omitted.

        7) Ambiguity is resolved against the author of the language.

        8) In construing an agreement of doubtful meaning, the doubt will be resolved against the party who made the proposal that was accepted.

        9) Ambiguous language will be construed reasonably and realistically.

      10) Practices consistent with the agreement remain effective unless the contract expressly provides otherwise.

      11) It is generally assumed that every phrase or proviso was inserted for a reason.

      12) An interpretation that makes a nullity of any clause or portion of a clause will be avoided.

13) A contract is construed as a whole; to determine the meaning of any part, it is generally necessary to consider its relation to all other parts.

14) The parties' intentions will be judged by the final form of expression, against a backdrop of statements or arguments, or positions advanced during the bargaining.

15) If either party relies upon and seeks a benefit based upon an oral or side agreement, that party has the burden of proving the existence of the agreement and its terms.

16) *Expressio unius est exclusio alterius.* Where a clause expressly describes a particular act or thing to which it shall apply, an irrefutable inference is drawn that what is omitted or not included was intended to be omitted and excluded.

8. *The Arbitrator*—If the agreement does not name or provide for the method of selecting an arbitrator, it is suggested that the parties agree to choose from an AAA panel. The AAA submits the panel to each party, who has seven days from the mailing date in which to cross off names he objects to, number the remaining names indicating the order of his preference, and return the list to AAA. From among these persons who have been approved on both lists and in accordance with the designated order of mutual preference, AAA shall invite the acceptance of an arbitrator to serve. CPLR 7504 provides that if the agreement does not provide for an appointment of an arbitrator, or if the agreed upon method does not succeed, then upon application of a party, a court shall appoint an arbitrator.

9. *The Decision*—under the laws of New York, the decision of the arbitrator may be confirmed by a court within one year of its delivery (CPLR 7510), and judgment entered upon the confirmation (CPLR 7514).

10. *Vacating*—review powers of a court are restricted. You will not be permitted to reargue the merits of the arbitration. If this could be done, the arbitration would be a meaningless gesture. A court has very limited powers to set aside (vacate) an arbitration decision. A court may vacate the decision where the rights of a party were prejudiced by:

a. Corruption, fraud, or misconduct in procuring the award, or

b. Partiality of an arbitrator appointed as a neutral, or

c. An arbitrator exceeded his power or so imperfectly executed it, that a final and definite award upon the subject was not made (the most popular ground), or

d. Failure to follow the procedure of Article 75 of the CPLR, unless the party waives his right to object (CPLR 7511).

11. *Expenses of the Arbitration Proceeding.* Many people consider the way to cut down the settlement of grievances by arbitration is to provide in the agreement that the costs of the proceeding will be shared equally by the parties. If the agreement provides that the AAA Rules are to govern the process of the grievance, the fees and expenses of the proceeding will be shared equally by the parties. If there has been no such agreement regarding fees and expenses, then the arbitrator will determine who will pay them (CPLR 7513). Failure to provide in the agreement for the sharing of these costs may invite grievances with the hope that the charging party will be able to convince the arbitrator not only that his cause is just, but that the other side should be required to pay all fees and expenses. Sometimes such a "flyer" pays off. Fees and expenses of this proceeding can be substantial.

Although the foregoing steps are prescribed when a grievance occurs, a better way to handle a grievance is to avoid it entirely. This can be done by choosing the language of your agreement carefully and by fully understanding its consequences and ramifications. A contract is not to be entered into lightly, particularly when internal machinery for policing its enforcement by binding third-party arbitration has been included within that contract.

\*            \*            \*

John Hogan is an attorney in the law firm of Pearis, Resseguie, Hogan & Kline in Binghamton, N.Y. He has had long experience in the field of labor relations. Mr. Hogan has served as labor counsel and negotiator to numerous boards of education in the Southern Tier, and has been a consultant to the N.Y. State School Boards Association.

# Discussion Questions

1. The article deals only with arbitration of a grievance. What other grievance resolution procedures are available to the parties in dispute? How do they compare with each other and with arbitration as effective tools for resolving grievances?

2. When and under what circumstances might it be better not to contest a grievance?

3. Discuss the role of past practice in grievance adjudication. How might past practices affect the current contract and lead to present grievances?

*Reprinted from Journal of Collective Negotiations in the Public Sector, Winter, 1972*

# CHAPTER 14

# The Impact of Statutory Law on Contract Interpretation in Public Education Grievance Arbitration

**KURT H. DECKER**

## Introduction

Throughout recent years the rapidly changing statutory framework has played an important role in developing the right of teachers to organize and bargain collectively. Within this statutory framework grievance arbitration is the "very heart" of the collective bargaining process.[1] It is responsible for defining the day-to-day relation-

---

[1] The grievance arbitration process has been described as being: "at the very heart of the system of industrial self-government. Arbitration is the means of solving the unforeseeable by molding a system of private law for all the problems which may arise and to provide for their solution in a way which will generally accord with the variant needs and desires of the parties. The processing of the disputes through the grievance machinery is actually a vehicle by which meaning and content is given to the collective bargaining agreement. . . . The grievance procedure is, in other words, a part of the continuous collective bargaining process." United Steelworkers v. Warrior & Gulf Navigation Co., 363 U.S. 574, 581 (1960).

ship between teachers and school officials. In addition, grievance arbitration has been based on a variety of statutes and directives, with many providing for either advisory or binding arbitration.[2]

Under a contract, the bargaining parties can determine the arbitrator's limits for reaching a decision. However, there is a limit to the authority that may be properly delegated to the arbitrator [1].[3] This is determined by the applicable statutes. Therefore, unless limitations on the scope of matters submitted through grievance arbitration are specifically noted in the contract, the arbitrator is afforded as much discretion as the statutes permit.

With the aforementioned in mind, recent judicial interpretations of grievance arbitration in public education are examined below. The areas to be considered are the arbitrator's authority and the arbitrability of the subject matter.

## Analysis of Recent Decisions Involving Grievance Arbitration in Public Education

Once a valid agreement providing for grievance arbitration has been entered into, any controversy between the parties that is within the scope of these provisions must proceed to arbitration [2]. The only instances where a court will enjoin arbitration are: (1) where there is fraud or duress in the inception of the contract; (2) where there is no *bona fide* dispute between the parties; (3) where the performance that is the subject of the demand is prohibited by statute; and (4) where a condition precedent to arbitration under the contract has not been met [3]. If the issue is solely one of construction or interpretation, it is for the arbitrators and not the courts to decide [4].

There is an accepted rule that where a labor agreement contains an arbitration provision, it is presumed that questions of arbitrability are for the arbitrator to decide [5]. This presumption of arbitrability applies equally to questions of substance and procedure [5]. In addition, it has been held that the court's function is limited to finding that a dispute does in fact exist [5]. Thus, if a

---

[2] The following states require grievance arbitration provisions to be included in the collective bargaining agreement: Alaska, Hawaii, Kansas, Maine, Massachusetts, Minnesota, Nebraska, Nevada, New Jersey, New York, Oklahoma, Oregon, Pennsylvania, Rhode Island, South Dakota, and Vermont. For a brief discussion of the aforementioned statutes see *ABA, Labor Relations Law Committee Report II*, 1973, pp. 296-298.

[3] The collective bargaining agreement cannot by its own pronouncement vest discretion in an arbitrator where that discretion has been specifically delegated to the Board of Education by the laws of the state [1].

dispute exists, the arbitrator and not the court, must examine the merits of the dispute itself. Moreover, this rule has been specifically applied to contracts providing for grievance arbitration that were executed by school districts and teacher associations [6].

It is only where the parties have employed language that clearly rebuts this presumption of arbitrability[4] that the matter may be determined by the courts [7]. Thus, it is clear that the function of the court will be to determine whether the parties to the contract agreed to submit specific issues to arbitration [8]. The courts accomplish this by looking at the wording of the collective bargaining agreement.

With this in mind, recent decisions involving judicial interpretation of the effect of a state statute on public education grievance arbitration are analyzed. The first area of focus is the arbitrator's authority.

## THE ARBITRATOR'S AUTHORITY

The function of grievance arbitration in contract administration is to resolve disputes arising out of the collective bargaining agreement. An arbitrator has no power to add, subtract, or modify any provision of the collective bargaining agreement. His task is to determine whether a particular pattern of conduct constitutes a violation of the collective bargaining agreement. In short, the arbitrator applies the existing contract to the facts of the case to determine whether a violation has occurred.

In determining whether an arbitrator has operated within his authority, the court will examine the collective bargaining agreement for guidance. Moreover, the court will generally recognize that deference is to be given to arbitration awards [9]. However, where the arbitration clause has been framed in restrictive rather than broad language, an arbitrator will have exceeded his authority if his award is not within the parameters of the collective bargaining agreement. In addition, an arbitrator exceeds his authority when he purports to exercise authority that has been vested by statute in another body.

An arbitrator's authority in making an award favoring the teacher association's position on duty-free lunch periods was questioned in *Board of Educ. v. Champaign Educ. Assn.* [9]. The basis of the court's decision was that the arbitrator exceeded his authority in making the award. In rendering its opinion, the court

---

[4] *E.g.*, by stating that an issue pertaining to either procedure or substance is not to be determined by arbitration.

recognized that deference is to be given to arbitration awards, especially in the area of labor relations [9]. However, here the arbitration agreement was framed in restrictive rather than broad language.[5] The court reasoned that the School Code provision on lunch periods did not conflict with the agreement, but was completely independent of the agreement. Therefore, it was outside the power of the arbitrator [9].

A similar ruling was made by the court in *Belanger v. Matteson* [10]. Here the arbitration board ousted a teacher selected by the school committee to be the business department head at the high school. In his place the arbitration board installed the grievant. In reversing the arbitration board reasoned that the School Committee is vested with the power and authority to select teachers. Moreover, under Rhode Island statutes, the School Committee could not delegate the jurisdiction conferred upon it in the absence of specific legislative authority to do so [11]. The court found that the arbitration board exercised authority that had been vested exclusively in the School Committee by statute. Therefore, since the arbitration board did not have the authority to hire and assign teachers, its award was in excess of its statutory powers [12].

Thus, it is the agreement between the bargaining parties that fixes the conditions, limitations, and restrictions to be observed by the arbitrator in making his award. The arbitrator in turn must give full faith and credit to the language of the collective bargaining agreement at the time of the dispute. Moreover, it should be recognized that the language of the collective bargaining agreement binds the school board, the teachers' association, the teachers, and the arbitrator.

It is not within the arbitrator's scope of authority to decide whether a particular contract clause is wise or undesirable. His job is to apply the language of the collective bargaining agreement as he finds it in a particular dispute. For an arbitrator to follow any other course of action would be a breach of faith to the bargaining parties. The arbitrator must regard the collective bargaining contract as a final authority. Moreover, he must give it his full respect in making his award. However, if a case goes against a party because of unclear or amgibuous contract language, the responsibility for this adverse state of affairs lies not with the arbitrator. Rather, it lies with the parties who negotiated the contract and authored the wording.

[5] Step 4 of the agreement's grievance procedure contained the arbitration clause and stated that: "The arbitrator shall make his decision strictly on the terms of the agreement and shall make no decision contrary to, or in conflict with the agreement nor in violation with existing laws [9, p. 2042, 2043]."

## THE ARBITRABILITY OF THE SUBJECT MATTER

Both federal and state decisions have made it clear that it is the function of the court to determine whether the parties to a collective bargaining contract have agreed to submit specific issues to arbitration [13]. This relation of the courts to arbitration was specified by the Supreme Court in the *Steelworkers* Triology [14]. These cases established the following propositions: (1) the function of the court is limited "to ascertaining whether the party seeking arbitration is making a claim which on its face is governed by the contract [15];" (2) doubts as to the coverage of the arbitration clause should be resolved in favor of arbitration [16]; and (3) an arbitrator's award, though it must be based on the collective bargaining agreement, must be enforced by the courts even if his interpretation of the contract would differ from the court [17].

Since the issue of arbitrability is for the courts, the court must determine both whether the parties agreed to arbitrate and what arbitrable issues are included in the agreement. Hence, it is evident that the court will look to see what is embraced in the agreement to arbitrate. The clause may be narrow or broad, but it is up to the parties to delimit the area of arbitration.

A recurring question of arbitrability in public education has involved the status of probationary teachers. In *Central School District No. 1 v. Three Village Teachers' Assn.*, a probationary teacher sought arbitration of her dismissal [18]. The legal effect of the dismissal was a denial of tenure. Here the labor agreement between the parties precluded arbitration for the dismissal [18]. Furthermore, the agreement specifically provided that the question of whether tenure was improperly denied was not a grievance and was not subject to arbitration [18]. The court, in reaching its decision, considered *the Matter of Howard & Co. v. Daley* [19]. In *Matter of Howard & Co.*, the court said that "arbitration is essentially a matter of contract and a party cannot be required to submit to arbitration any dispute which he has not agreed to submit" [19]. Thus, in the instant case the court denied the request for arbitration on the basis that the parties had not agreed to submit such issues to arbitration [20]. Moreover, the court held that arbitration of this issue was barred by a New York statute which specified that services of nontenured teachers may be terminated at any time during the probationary period without a hearing [20].

A similar result was reached by the court in *Central School Dist. No. 3 v. Faculty Assn.* [21]. However, this time the court found that an issue is not arbitrable where the legislature has vested authority with another body [21]. Once again the issue of tenure and a probationary teacher was before the court. The court proceeded on a motion of the school district for an order staying the arbitration demanded by the probationary teacher. Here the collective bargaining agreement defined a grievance as "any complaint by a teacher or group of teachers based on an alleged violation, misinterpretation or inequitable application of existing State laws, Board policies, administrative procedures and regulations or this agreement" [21]. In formulating its decision, the court reasoned that even if the definition of a "grievance" was broad enough to encompass the grievance, the collective bargaining agreement cannot by his own pronouncement vest discretion in an arbitrator to decide an issue involving tenure [21]. That function was specifically delegated to the Board of Education by state law [21]. Thus, where the legislature explicitly delegates authority to another body an arbitrator lacks power and the issue is not arbitrable [22].

On the other hand, it appears that probationary teachers may utilize contractual grievance arbitration procedures where they specifically provide provisions for the handling of disciplinary grievances [23]. Moreover, an issue is deemed arbitrable where the board fails to comply with contractual provisions providing for the evaluation of probationary teachers before dismissal [24]. Of course, in these latter instances, it must be remembered that the collective bargaining agreements contained specific provisions for the benefit of probationary teachers. Thus, provisions dealing with discipline and periodic evaluations of probationary teachers prior to dismissal appear to be arbitrable. However, if the collective bargaining agreements had not contained such clauses, the issues would not have been arbitrable.

Considerable attention has also been focused upon tenured teachers and the arbitrability of their disputes. As with probationary teachers, the issue of discipline has also caused problems for tenured teachers. It has been questioned on the basis of whether it is a "term or condition" of employment [25].[6] In *Board of Education v. Associated Teachers (Huntington)*, the court considered whether a school board lacks the power to enter into a contract providing for arbitration of disputes involving the discipline of tenured teachers [26]. The court held that a board of education

---

[6] Generally, teacher organizations have given the term "conditions of employment" an extremely broad meaning, while boards of education have tried to restrict the term to preserve their management prerogatives and policy-making powers. While there are many nebulous areas, boards should not be required to enter negotiations on matters that are predominantly matters of educational policy, management prerogatives, or statutory duties of the boards of education [25].

has authority under New York's Taylor Law to enter into a collective bargaining agreement authorizing arbitration of disputes concerning the discipline of tenured teachers [26]. Such a provision constitutes a "term or condition" of employment within the meaning of the Taylor Law [26]. Also, the school board is required by the Taylor Law to negotiate with the association concerning "terms and conditions" of employment and to incorporate any understanding into the contract [26]. The court explained that there is no reason to infer that the legislature intended the provisions of the State Tenure Law to deprive unions of the right to represent employees in disciplinary grievances [26]. Moreover, an arbitrator is no less qualified than the board of education to decide whether teachers should be dismissed for "incompetency or misconduct" [26]. In addition, absence of a specific statutory provision expressly authorizing a school board to provide for a particular "term or condition" does not preclude the board of education from doing so [26].

Thus, such a grievance provision, as discussed in *Board of Education v. Associated Teachers (Huntington)*, assures tenured teachers that no disciplinary action will be taken against them without just cause [26]. Also, any dispute as to the existence of such cause may be submitted to arbitration. Such a provision is commonly found in collective bargaining agreements in the private and public sectors. It carries out federal and state policy favoring arbitration as a means of resolving labor disputes [27].

Failure to provide an applicable contract provision covering the discharge of guidance counselors was considered in *Board of Education v. United Teachers of Northport* [28]. Again, the court ruled that a grievance that does not involve "interpretation, meaning, or application" of a specific contract provision is not arbitrable [28]. Other decisions treating the arbitrability of issues that have been restricted or omitted by the collective bargaining agreement include: (1) the resignation of teachers [29];[7] (2) inclusion of head teachers in a bargaining unit [30];[8] and (3) disputes concerning salary and insurance benefits under a reopening provision [31].[9] Cases such as the aforementioned point out the importance for both teacher associations and boards of education of including suf-

[7] The issue is not arbitrable where there is nothing in the contract relating to termination or employment or reinstatement after resignation [29].
[8] The inclusion of head teachers in a bargaining unit is not arbitrable. An arbitrators authority is limited to the express language of the contract [30].
[9] Not an arbitrable grievance, since the contract required arbitration only of disputes concerning its meaning, interpretation, or application. The present dispute concerned a new provision to be inserted in a contract [31].

ficient contractual provisions. Such provisions should deal with the handling of a wide variety of grievances. Only in this manner can teachers and boards of education protect themselves from adverse results occurring through inept grievance arbitration procedures.

On the other hand, school boards must be cognizant that they cannot delegate authority to arbitrators that they possess by statute. This can be illustrated by the court's treatment of *Board of Education v. Rockford Education Association* [32]. Here arbitration resulted over the failure of the school board to select a teacher for promotion to an administrative position [32]. The court held that this matter was not arbitrable. It reasoned that the school board may not delegate to an arbitrator matters of discretion that are vested in it by statute [32]. Thus, it can be seen that a school board may not, through a collective bargaining agreement or otherwise, delegate to an arbitrator those matters reserved to it by statute [33].

A unique decision, holding issues arbitrable, involved the situation where the parties were in the midst of negotiations and the current contract expired [34]. In *Board of Education v. Connetquot Teachers' Assn.*, it appeared as if the prior year's contract had expired and the status of a "memorandum of agreement" reached by the negotiating parties was undetermined at the time the grievance was submitted to arbitration [34]. The court ruled that the teachers' association is entitled to have the grievance submitted to arbitration, even assuming no contract existed. This was based upon the rationale that public employees are prohibited from striking under New York's Taylor Law [34]. Therefore, such employees must be protected during the hiatus between the expiration date of an old contract and the signing of a new one [34].

From the aforementioned decisions, it can be inferred that the emerging rule in determining the arbitrability of particular disputes is whether the agreement in "carefully drafted words" clearly and unambiguously excludes arbitration for that particular grievance. Thus, where there is no controlling provision in the agreement prohibiting arbitration of the grievance, the issue will most likely be considered arbitrable.

## Conclusions

Public education provides an excellent environment for the development of a case-by-case method of defining the scope of collective bargaining [35]. The potential overlap of management functions with bargainable subjects leads to some rather fine line-drawing. This is done by labor boards as they attempt to strike a proper balance "between the duty of elected officials to make decisions for the entire electorate and the statutory right of employees to negotiate items directly affecting terms and conditions of employment" [35].

It can be seen that collective bargaining agreements in public education have steadily gained specificity. This is especially true with regard to aspects of the grievance arbitration procedure. This increasing specificity in grievance arbitration has occurred through a costly process of learning from experience the problems that arise when the phraseology covering such matters is not carefully drafted. The unpleasant result is often expensive and time-consuming litigation.

In essence, the grievance arbitration process is a mere extension of the collective bargaining process. The rules are the same here as in negotiations, namely the teachers' association will go after all that the "traffic will reasonably bear."

Thus, school boards charged with administering public education labor agreements would be well-advised to examine their particular state statute for grievance arbitration details, if any. Then the collective bargaining agreement should be formulated with sufficient procedural specificity. In this way the authority of the arbitrator can be clearly defined and the scope of arbitrable grievances will be better understood.

## REFERENCES

1. *Central School District No. 3 of the Town of Cortlandt v. Central School District No. 3 Faculty Association*, 75 Misc.2d 521, 348 N.Y.S.2d 295 (1973).
2. *Matter of Exercycle Corp.*, 9 N.Y.2d 329, 214 N.Y.S.2d 353 (1961).
3. *Belanger v. Matteson*, 85 L.R.R.M. 2924 (R. I. Super. Ct. 1974).
4. *Matter of Exercycle Corp.*, 9 N.Y.2d 329, 214 N.Y.S.2d 353, 358 (1961).
5. *Matter of Long Is. Lbr. Co.*, 15 N.Y.2d 380, 259 N.Y.S.2d 142, 146, 147 (1965).
6. *Central School Dist. No. 1 v. Litz*, 60 Misc.2d 1009, 304 N.Y.S.2d 372 (1969).
7. *John Wiley & Sons, Inc. v. Livingstons*, 376 U.S. 543 (1964); *Atkinson v. Sinclair Refining Co.*, 370 U.S. 238 (1962); *United Steelworkers of America v. American Mfg. Co.*, 363 U.S. 564 (1960).
8. *United Steelworkers of America v. American Mfg. Co.*, 363 U.S. 564 (1960).
9. *Board of Educ. v. Champaign Educ. Assn.*, 85 L.R.R.M. 2041, 2043 (Ill. App. Ct. 1973).
10. *Belanger v. Matteson*, 85 L.R.R.M. 2924 (R. I. Super. Ct. 1974).
11. See *Dawson v. Clark*, 93 R.I. 457, 176 A.2d 732 (1962).

12. *Belanger v. Matteson*, 85 L.R.R.M. 2924 (R.I. Super. Ct. 1974).
13. *United Steelworkers v. American Mfg. Co.*, 363 U.S. 564 (1960).
14. *United Steelworkers v. American Mfg. Co.*, 363 U.S. 564 (1960); *United Steelworkers v. Warrior & Gulf Navigation Co.*, 363 U.S. 574 (1960); *United Steelworkers v. Enterprise Wheel & Car Corp.*, 363 U.S. 593 (1960).
15. *United Steelworkers v. American Mfg. Co.*, 363 U.S. 564, 568 (1960).
16. *United Steelworkers v. Warrior & Gulf Navigation Co.*, 363 U.S. 574 (1960).
17. *United Steelworkers v. Enterprise Wheel & Car Corp.*, 363 U.S. 593 (1960).
18. *Central School District No. 1 v. Three Village Teachers' Assn.*, 39 App. Div.2d 466, 336 N.Y.S.2d 656, 657 (1972).
19. *Matter of Howard & Co. v. Daley*, 27 N.Y.2d 285, 317, 330 N.Y.S.2d 326, 330 (1971).
20. *Central School District No. 1 v. Three Village Teachers' Assn.*, 39 App. Div.2d 466, 336 N.Y.S.2d 656, 659 (1972).
21. *Central School Dist. No. 3 v. Faculty Assn.*, 75 Misc.2d 521, 348 N.Y.S.2d 295, 296 (1973).
22. See also *Lehman v. Board of Education*, 78 L.R.R.M. 2327 (N.Y. Sup. Ct. 1971).
23. *School District v. Lester*, 80 L.R.R.M. 3009 (Mich. Cir. Ct. 1972).
24. *Chautauqua Bd. of Educ. v. Teachers' Assn.*, 84 L.R.R.M. 2772 (N.Y. App. Div. 1973).
25. *School District of Seward Education Association v. School District of Seward*, 188 Neb. 772, 199 N.W.2d 752 (1972).
26. *Board of Education v. Associated Teachers (Huntington)*, 30 N.Y.2d 122, 331 N.Y.S.2d 17-25 (1972).
27. Ida Klaus, "The Evolution of a Collective Bargaining Relationship in Public Education," *Michigan Law Review*, LXVII (1969), 1033, 1040-41.
28. *Board of Education v. United Teachers of Northport*, 82 L.R.R.M. 3052 (N.Y. Sup. Ct. 1972).
29. *Board of Educ. v. Wittman*, 82 L.R.R.M. 2671 (N.Y. Sup. Ct. 1972).
30. *Board of Education v. Teachers Local 1760*, 83 L.R.R.M. 2990 (N.Y. Sup. Ct. 1973).
31. *Teachers' Assn. v. Bd. of Education, Union Free School District No. 4*, 78 L.R.R.M. 2879 (N.Y. Sup. Ct. 1971).
32. *Board of Education v. Rockford Education Association*, 3 Ill. App.3d 1090, 280 N.E.2d 286, 288 (1972).
33. *Dunellen Board of Educ. v. Educ. Assn.*, 85 L R.R.M. 2131 (N.J. Sup. Ct. 1973).
34. *Board of Education v. Connetquot Teachers' Assn.*, 81 L.R.R.M. 2253-2254 (N.Y. Sup. Ct. 1972).
35. Harry T. Edwards, "The Emerging Duty to Bargain in the Public Sector," LXXI, *Michigan Law Review*, (1973), 885, 919, 920.

*     *     *

Kurt Decker is the former Director of the Pennsylvania School Study Council's project concerning the impact of collective bargaining upon public education in Pennsylvania. He is currently Assistant Attorney General in the Pennsylvania Governor's office.

# Discussion Questions

1. Discuss an arbitrator's role in resolving a contract dispute. What are the parameters of his/her role?
2. Discuss arbitrability as it applies to probationary teachers. When are they considered covered by the existing contract, and when are they excluded, according to cases cited here?
3. The scope of bargaining has been defined so far on a case-by-case basis. Why should this be so? Can a single law cover the entire range of possible circumstances?
4. How do management rights conflict or agree with employee demands in public education?

*Reprinted from Journal of Collective Negotiations in the Public Sector, Winter, 1975*

# CHAPTER 15

# How Impartial Is Impartial Arbitration when it Involves Public School Teachers?

**DR. HARRY KERSHEN**
*Negotiator and Personnel Administrator*
*Seaford Public School District*

## Purpose of the Study

The purpose of this study was to examine the awards rendered by arbitrators in grievance disputes with public school teachers to determine whether a significant number of awards were weighted in favor of either labor or management. A second purpose was to determine whether some arbitrators were consistent in their findings for one of the parties (names of the arbitrators were deleted to preserve anonymity). The fundamental goal underlying this investigation was to evaluate whether arbitration, as presently practiced, is an impartial method of adjudication in public education.

### LIMITATIONS

The study was limited to arbitration awards in the State of New York that were recorded by the American Arbitration Association and the Public Employment Relations Board and that affected only public school teachers. A perusal of the arbitration files at the American Arbitration Association revealed that 1971 was the first year the AAA began collecting this type of data. The study is limited to awards on file that were made from the inception of record keeping in 1971 thru November, 1974. The files at the Public Employment Relations Board (PERB) are filed by category and cover the period from its inception of record keeping until May, 1974.

A further limitation is the absence of any attempt to investigate in detail the substantive issues in the cases under arbitration. The only concern of this study was to quantify the conclusions.

## SIGNIFICANCE

The significance of the study lies in its potential aid to school boards in the selection of arbitrators by making boards aware of arbitration award patterns. Although the scope of the study was limited with respect to the substantive issues, it was felt that the material collected would be of value to parties selecting an arbitrator.

Table 1 shows that the decisions or awards by arbitrators favor the unions slightly more often than they favor the employers. Of the 363 cases, 51% sustained the union position. If the 20 cases of "no decision" are eliminated, the percentage of cases favoring the union increases to 54%.

Table 1. Results of Arbitration Cases

| Filed with | # of cases | In favor of union | | In favor of district | | No decision | |
|---|---|---|---|---|---|---|---|
| AAA | 335 | 179 | (53%) | 147 | (44%) | 9 | ( 3%) |
| PERB | 101 | 49 | (49%) | 40 | (40%) | 12 | (12%) |
| Total | 436 | 228 | (52%) | 187 | (43%) | 21 | ( 5%) |
| Total (Eliminating "no decision") | 415 | 228 | (55%) | 187 | (45%) | — | |

Table 2 is self-explanatory. It is a graphic view of the more active arbitrators and their patterns of awards. The list contains those arbitrators who have written six or more awards, either with AAA or PERB or a combination of the two.

Table 2.  Pattern of Arbitration by Active Arbitrators
(6 or more decisions)

| Arbitrator | In favor of union | In favor of district | No decision |
|---|---|---|---|
| A | 3 | 8 | |
| B | 5 | 4 | |
| C | 10 | 3 | |
| D | 2 | 5 | |
| E | 22 | 10 | 1 |
| F | 5 | 2 | |
| G | 7 | 2 | 1 |
| H | 3 | 2 | 1 |
| I | 6 | 4 | |
| J | 7 | 1 | |
| K | 5 | 7 | |
| L | 5 | 7 | 3 |
| M | 8 | 5 | |
| N | 5 | 10 | 1 |
| O | 6 | 2 | |
| P | 1 | 5 | 1 |
| Q | 3 | 3 | |
| R | 4 | 5 | |
| S | 7 | 3 | |
| T | 3 | 6 | |
| U | 3 | 4 | 1 |
| V | 4 | 4 | |
| W | 4 | 2 | |
| X | 5 | 8 | |
| Y | 17 | 3 | |
| Z | 6 | 5 | |

Table 3 is a listing of AAA arbitration awards for the three-year period, 1971-1974. The table is divided into two groups because the American Arbitration Association maintains two offices in New York State. The New York City office includes all the suburban counties that comprise the metropolitan area, while the Syracuse office handles disputes in the remainder of the State.

## What Inferences Can be Drawn?

In view of the foregoing findings, one may suspect that union negotiators possess greater skills in the canons of construction when reducing an agreement to a written contract. This assumption is

Table 3.  AAA Composite

| New York Office area | Year | # of cases | In favor of union | In favor of district | Tie |
|---|---|---|---|---|---|
| New York City | 1971 | 15 | 8 | 7 | |
| | 1972 | 12 | 5 | 6 | 1 |
| | 1973 | 8 | 3 | 5 | |
| | | **35** | **16** | **18** | **1** |
| Nassau | 1971 | 6 | 3 | 3 | |
| | 1972 | 17 | 5 | 12 | |
| | 1973 | 33 | 18 | 14 | 1 |
| | | **56** | **26** | **29** | **1** |
| Suffolk | 1971 | 7 | 5 | 1 | 1 |
| | 1972 | 22 | 11 | 10 | 1 |
| | 1973 | 29 | 15 | 12 | 2 |
| | | **58** | **31** | **23** | **4** |
| Westchester | 1971 | 4 | 3 | 1 | |
| | 1972 | 20 | 12 | 8 | |
| | 1973 | 18 | 12 | 5 | 1 |
| | | **42** | **27** | **14** | **1** |
| Rockland | 1971 | | | | |
| | 1972 | 12 | 7 | 5 | |
| | 1973 | 3 | 2 | 1 | |
| | | **15** | **9** | **6** | |
| Dutchess | 1971 | 2 | 2 | | |
| | 1972 | 4 | 4 | | |
| | 1973 | 1 | | 1 | |
| | | **7** | **6** | **1** | |
| Other Counties | 1971 | | | | |
| | 1972 | 5 | 3 | 1 | 1 |
| | 1973 | 4 | 1 | 3 | |
| | | **9** | **4** | **4** | **1** |
| Syracuse Office | 1971 | 2 | 2 | | |
| | 1972 | 29 | 15 | 14 | |
| | 1973 | 82 | 43 | 38 | 1 |
| | | **113** | **60** | **52** | **1** |
| TOTAL | | **335** | **179** | **147** | **9** |

questionable since management has the resources to retain highly trained personnel who possess equal skill.

Perhaps, then, union representatives present a stronger case at the arbitration hearing. Here again the assumption is incorrect. There is no reason to believe that employers' representatives are not as skilled and meticulous in the preparation of a case and as eloquent in the presentation of a case, as the unions' representatives.

Well, then, perhaps most minor issues are resolved at one of the grievance levels below arbitration. Unresolved grievances must therefore be a clear-cut violation of the contract; otherwise, the union wouldn't be pursuing the grievance. If this were so, management wouldn't be awarded in 43% of the cases (or 46%—see Table 1). Obviously, this assumption is fallacious.

Perhaps some arbitrators are not as objective as others. Or perhaps some arbitrators are prejudicial in their philosophical views toward one of the two parties. One may well question the impartiality of an arbitrator who consistently finds for one of the parties. It is difficult to assume that it is a coincidence that certain arbitrators consistently have clear-cut cases favoring the same party or, perhaps it may be that labor knows *whom* to select.

## Conclusion

The history of labor in America has depicted the American working man as being exploited by the greed of the industrialists and the capitalistic system. With the advent of collective bargaining and the inception of the National Labor Relations Board, the American worker gained the opportunity to bargain for his labor in the open market place. The Wagner Act was enacted during the depression years and the ranks of labor swelled. World War II followed shortly thereafter and due to the war effort strikes and labor strife were largely put aside. Resolution of differences was resolved by means of arbitration. The art of this impasse technique was utilized extensively by various governmental agencies during this period.

Most veteran arbitrators, those most in demand and most frequently used, are products of the depression years and were witness to the abuses inflicted upon the working class.

How does this information apply to arbitration in the public sector? Well, public servants in New York State were excluded from the Wagner Act in 1935. Collective bargaining and the right to mutually determine wages and terms and conditions of employment were denied to this class until 1967. For many years the school teacher was depicted as underpaid and overworked and lagging behind private industry in benefits and working conditions. In spite of the fact that teachers may now bargain collectively, the unions have perpetuated the image of the underdog, preferring to claim that equality still eludes this class of workers regardless of existing facts. The unions contend that the right to strike does not exist, that exploitation of workers by management continues. Where can the union turn for equity with the right to strike denied? The answer lies in arbitration. It is against this backdrop that arbitrators enter the arena. Does the traditional concept of harrassed teacher dominate the thinking of the arbitrator? Is the arbitrator psychologically predisposed to view the teachers' grievance as legitimate and worthy? Is the arbitrator applying the private sector industrial experience to public school teachers? Is the arbitrator utilizing the experience he gained in governmental agencies in evaluating disputes in public education?

A general feeling exists among managerial personnel in public education that a board of education cannot get an even break. Arbitrators apply a strict contract interpretation yardstick to management, such as "in the absence of specific language," yet adopt a liberal attitude toward union complaints. For public employers the great hope of arbitration has merely become an exercise in futility. The statistics speak for themselves.

What does all this mean? The strike for public employees is still prohibited. An instrument of finality is still being sought and various forms of arbitration are being promoted as viable strike substitutes. What many have found is not a failure of the arbitration process *per se*, but a lack of understanding of public education by most arbitrators, and a possible built-in bias.

Arbitrators must be schooled in the nuances of public education as well as being made knowledgeable in regard to the various educational laws; the civil service laws, rules and regulations; and the education commissioner's regulations as they apply to interpretations of teacher contracts. The continued application of the industrial sector method of contract interpretation to public education will demolish whatever confidence remains with respect to arbitration.

As for the arbitrator's bias, school boards should not use arbitrators whose record reflects one-sidedness. Each arbitrator's entire "track" record, including the substantive issues of the cases heard and his analysis, should be available for review. This information does not presently exist. A well-organized statewide teacher's union is in a position to maintain such a record for itself. Employers are not that well organized. Perhaps the American Arbitration Association and the Public Employment Relations Board should be authorized, or required, to do research and publish information of this nature.

## Discussion Questions

1. How important is it for arbitrators to be consistent in their decisions?
2. What other factors beyond bias might influence an arbitrator's decision? Discuss the pros and cons of the other factors and their effect on an arbitrator's award.
3. How are arbitrators selected by the parties? Do you see this process as viable? How might improvements in the selection process be made?
4. If both parties to a dispute seek arbitrators whose "track record" shows fairness to their sides, what problems would result?

*Reprinted from Journal of Collective Negotiations in the Public Sector, Summer, 1975*

# CHAPTER 16

# The Canadian Approach to Grievance Adjudication in the Public Sector

**E. EDWARD HERMAN**
*Professor of Economics*
*University of Cincinnati*

On March 13, 1967, employer-employee relations in the Canadian Federal Public Service entered a new era. On this date, the newly enacted Public Service Staff Relations Act or the PSSR Act came into force. The purpose of the statute was to provide the federal public sector with a system of collective bargaining. The Canadian law has many interesting components that warrant close scrutiny and evaluation. However, the scope of this article is confined to the examination of the elaborate grievance and adjudication procedure incorporated in the PSSR Act.

In the private sector, an employee's right to file a grievance and to go to arbitration is based on the terms of the labor contract. Under the Canadian legislation, however the right of federal public employees to grieve and for certain type of cases to proceed to adjudication is incorporated in the statute itself, and is present with or without the existence of a collective agreement. The grievance and adjudication procedures governing employees working for the Canadian federal government are incorporated in two basic documents: the PSSR Act and the Regulations and Rules of Procedure issued by the Public Service Staff Relations Board or the PSSRB. The Board is responsible for the administration of the PSSR Act.

## The Grievance Procedure

Section 90 of the PSSR Act permits any employee to submit a grievance concerning terms and conditions of employment where the complaint is related to application and interpretation of the following instruments: a provision of a statute, a regulation of a by-law, any document prepared by the employer, a provision of a collective agreement, or an arbitral award. Any grievance presented by an agrieved employee may move through all the steps of the grievance process established in accordance with the law. There are a number of limitations on an employee's right to utilize the grievance machinery. The right does not extend to areas where an "administrative procedure for redress is provided in or under an Act of Parliament;" also, where a collective agreement or an arbitral award is present the employee has to secure the approval and representation of a bargaining agent before he can file a complaint related to application or interpretation of these documents. The right to file a grievance is not restricted to employees who are in a bargaining unit. It also extends to persons who are not represented by a bargaining agent but who under the legislation have bargaining rights. The right to grieve also embraces persons who would be employees but for the fact that they are employed "in a managerial or confidential capacity [1]" and thus are excluded from the category of employees entitled to collective bargaining.

Under Section 99 of the Act the PSSR Board is vested with the authority to "make regulations in relation to the procedure for the presenting of grievances." Board regulations regarding grievance procedures do not apply to employees in a bargaining unit where the Board regulations are in conflict with the provisions of a collective agreement [2]. In accordance with the powers granted the Board in Section 99 of the Act, a very elaborate grievance and adjudication procedure has been enacted by the Board [3].

Section 37 of the Board's regulation requires the government to establish a grievance process "within each department or other portion of the public service." Schedule "A" of the PSSR Act specifies the appropriate subdivision of the labor force of the federal government for the purposes of the statute.

Section 38 (1) limits the grievance procedure to be established for public employees to not more than four levels. The employer has the responsibility to appoint an authorized representative to handle grievances at each level of the process [4]. The employer also has the responsibility for preparing a grievance form [5] which has to conform to a number of criteria stipulated in the regulations. To avoid delays in processing grievances, the PSSR Board rules stipulate the time limits at each step of the procedure [6]. After an employee has processed his grievance up to the final level of the grievance procedure and he is not satisfied with the outcome, and if his grievance falls within the scope of Section 91 of the PSSR Act, he has one more course of action open to him. He may refer his grievance to adjudication.

## The Adjudication Process

In the private sector the final step for unresolved grievances usually is final and binding arbitration. Under the Canadian Federal System this process is referred to as adjudication.

The PSSR Act states that "the Governor in Council on the recommendation of the Board shall appoint . . . officers, to be called adjudicators [7]." The function of these adjudicators would be "to hear and adjudicate upon grievances referred to adjudication under this Act [7]." One of the appointed officers is designated by the Governor in Council as the chief adjudicator.

Under the Canadian adjudication procedure there are three avenues of action open to an aggrieved employee [8]. One alternative is for the employee to request the chief adjudicator to select an adjudicator from the government appointed panel. Another method would be for the employee to ask for the formation of a board of adjudication. The creation of such a board is only possible where the employer does not voice any objections to its establishment [9]. Still another approach is for the parties to name an adjudicator in the collective agreement. Under such an arrangement the chief adjudicator has a statutory duty to refer the grievance to the adjudicator selected by the parties [10].

Under the PSSR Act only three specific categories of grievances may be referred to adjudication. The first two classifications are specified in Section 91, the third is covered in Section 98 of the Act. Section 91 confines adjudication to the following areas: "The interpretation or application . . . of a collective agreement or an arbitral award" or "disciplinary action resulting in discharge, suspension, or a financial penalty." Under Section 98 of the PSSR Act policy grievances regarding enforcement of obligations stemming from a collective agreement or an arbitration award can be referred by the employer or the bargaining agent to adjudication. These grievances cannot be filed on behalf of individual employees. According to the Act the determination of these grievances has to be undertaken personally by the chief adjudicator.

The PSSR Act became effective in March, 1967. Since the Act came into force until March 31, 1972, 607 [11] cases have been referred to adjudication. Out of these, 408 cases concerned interpretation and application of contract and arbitral awards under Section 91 (1) (a) of the Act, 180 cases involved discipline under Section 91 (1) (b), and 19 cases were filed under Section 98 of the statute. It is interesting to note that whereas the number of discipline cases declined from 45 in 1969-70 to 29 in 1971-72, the number of contract interpretation cases moved up from 95 in 1969-70 to 142 in 1971-72. The decline in disciplinary disputes suggests an improvement in the operation of the grievance procedure. The increase in interpretation cases is a trend directly related to the development of contractual relationships between the parties. The total number of contract interpretation cases, even though it increased from 95 to 142, is still relatively small considering the existence of over 100 bargaining units covered by agreements to which these interpretations applied [12]. The topics most frequently appearing in the contract interpretation grievances dealt with such subjects as "rates of pay, retroactivity, overtime and other premium payments, the scheduling of shifts and hours, and the conditions governing holidays, days of rest, and the granting of leave [12]."

Under the Canadian system the cost of adjudication is free to the parties as long as they utilize the person selected by the chief adjudicator from the panel of permanent adjudicators appointed by the government. Although Section 97 (2) (3) of the Canadian statute states that the PSSR Board may recover from the parties the cost of adjudication, such recapture has not been implemented [13] in the past.

According to the statute, when the parties name an adjudicator in a collective agreement, the method of his remuneration is to be incorporated into the contract. When this is not done, the adjudication cost has to be borne equally by the parties [14].

Presently, all adjudication decisions must be in writing and must give reasons [15]. At times two or more cases may be heard together. This can only be done when all the parties agree. This approach contributes to some efficiency by having one written decision affecting the combined grievances heard. Some grievances are adjudicated "on the basis of written representation only, which may be accompanied by a joint statement of facts and issues [15]. Again, a consent of all the parties is necessary for such a procedure. However, in most adjudication disputes there is a hearing open to the public at which all sides have an ample opportunity to present their respective positions. Although the hearings are not as formal as they would be in courts of law, the sessions are conducted in an orderly manner following the regulations and rules of procedure enacted by the PSSR Board.

Section 96 of the PSSR Act stipulates that the adjudicator must give both parties an opportunity to be heard. Following a hearing, the adjudicator renders a decision, copies of which go to all the interested parties. A copy of the decision is also deposited with the secretary of the PSSR Board. In situations where a case is heard by a board of adjudication instead of a single adjudicator, a majority decision is a decision of the board.

In cases where the decision of the adjudicator requires action by any of the parties, the PSSR Board may take the necessary steps to enforce the decision. The Board's powers to assure compliance with the decisions of an adjudicator are contained in Section 20 of the Act. The Board is authorized under this section to issue orders directing concurrence with adjudication decisions. In the event that the order is not complied with, the statute directs the Board to forward "to the minister through whom it reports to Parliament a copy of its order, a report of the circumstances and documents relevant thereto [16]." Within 15 days after receipt the minister has to present the report of the Board to Parliament. The machinery for enforcement of adjudication decisions seems to contain a strong dose of the force of public opinion. Since it is not likely that Parliament would take action in each instance of possible noncompliance with an adjudication award, the main safeguard against such occurrence would be the adverse publicity that would accompany any violation of adjudication decisions. In the public sector this could be a powerful weapon where both parties have to rely on the goodwill of the legislators.

## Evaluation of the Grievance and the Adjudication Process

The Canadian statute distinguishes between the rights of the individual employee and the rights and interest of all the members of the bargaining unit. An employee may file a personal grievance, but he cannot file a grievance "relating to the interpretation or application in respect to him of a provision of a collective agreement or an arbitral award unless he has the approval of and is represented by the bargaining agent [17]." There seems to be a great amount of wisdom in this approach. An employee should always have the right to grieve when he is personally affected by the action of the employer. An example of this would be a disciplinary discharge. But when a grievance of an employee could have an effect on all the people in the bargaining unit, the union that negotiated or inherited the agreement or obtained an arbitral award obviously should be a party to any action regarding such a contract or award. The bargaining agent also has the right to refuse to go to adjudication when in his opinion, such a course of action may be in the best interest of the employees in the bargaining unit.

Another important feature of the Canadian procedure is the ability of each employee, regardless of whether he is unionized or not, to avail himself of the grievance process. This approach can be beneficial not only from the point of view of the employee but also for management. The grievance machinery can serve as a channel of communication between labor and management. The procedure can alert the employer to problems of which he was unaware, it can contribute to higher productivity, and may lead to a more satisfied work force. At times the only thing an employee may really need is a forum to be heard. Permitting most employees to present grievances that they may have regarding any of the subjects covered by Section 91 of the Act has some therapeutic value. It provides the frustrated employee with an outlet for his anger and pent-up emotions. The Canadian open grievance procedure is beneficial to both parties and it can contribute to a better labor relations climate between labor and management.

In evaluating the Canadian adjudication system, the big question is where should the line be drawn between those grievances that can be adjudicated and those that fall outside the scope of the process. Under the present system, a grievance may go through all the steps of the grievance procedure and still remain unresolved. Some of these unresolved grievances are barred by statute from adjudication. Thus, without adjudication there is no alternative mechanism for resolving this particular type of grievances, regardless of their merits. These statutory limitations, obviously could contribute to future labor relations problems.

Section 91 (b) of the Act confines adjudication to "disciplinary action resulting in discharge, suspension, or a financial penalty." The statute does not define "disciplinary action." It is up to the adjudicators to decide in each case what falls under this particular heading. Clearly, grievors who seek adjudication attempt to classify each complaint as a discipline dispute. Adjudication decisions issued over the past few years created a body of principles as to what constitutes a disciplinary case. However, the adjudicators are not free agents and their activity is governed by statute. Professor Harry Arthurs, a past chief adjudicator, stated, "Disciplinary action is not infinitely flexible. We can't give everything with this term." Professor Arthurs referred to one case that he "read and wept yet could do nothing about a man who was a probationer in a lighthouse and apparently the senior lighthouse keeper was a man who had been too long alone with the waves and seagulls, and drove the poor fellow right around the bend [18]." The probationer wanted another chance at a different lighthouse. Unfortunately, Professor Arthurs did not think that the dispute came within the statutory powers vested with adjudicators and had to dismiss the case. Confining the adjudication process to the areas contained in Sections 91 and 98 of the statute may have been justified in the first few years of life of the Canadian Act. This approach had some merit when the parties were entering the unexplored territory of labor relations. Now with some experience behind them, it seems that the parties can afford to risk entering deeper waters and be permitted to submit a broader range of issues to adjudication. This obviously would require a legislative amendment of Section 91 and 98 of the Act.

The next area that warrants some examination is the concept of the government-appointed, permanent panel of neutral adjudicators. In the private sector, selection and availability of acceptable arbitrators can be a time-consuming task that can significantly delay the administration of justice. With a permanent panel of adjudicators the Canadian approach can be instrumental in speeding up the resolution of grievances [19]. Under this system the parties may not always get the person of their choice. However, over time they would probably end up with an acceptable average of favorable decisions. Although the Canadian system permits the parties the flexibility of seeking adjudication of grievances outside the permanent panel, it is unlikely that, under present conditions, the parties would be willing to move outside the formal adjudication process. Professor Arthurs [20] gives two reasons against such a development. The first one is cost; the second is uniformity of decisions. Since so far the public system has been free of charge, there was relatively little incentive for unions to seek alternative arrangements. This obviously could change if the PSSR Board decided to exercise its powers under Section 97 (2) of the Act and started charging the parties for adjudication services. One of the reasons probably responsible for the Board's reluctance to start charging is the possibility that such action may encourage the parties to hire outside adjudicators for resolution of their disputes. Having arbitrators hired by the parties risks disturbing the consistency in the decision-making process that is present with a permanent panel of adjudicators. It is presumably more desirable from the point of view of public interest to maintain a uniformity of adjudication decisions throughout the public service. In view of this, the position of the Board regarding adjudication expenses has some merit. However, if the parties began to abuse the adjudication process, the Board could be compelled to begin charging an adjudication fee. This abuse could take the form of minor disputes that should have been resolved at lower levels of the grievance procedure going to adjudication. Such a development would be unfortunate since it could lead to the disintegration of the presently utilized system of adjudication.

One could argue that too much uniformity in adjudication awards fostered by a permanent panel of adjudicators may not always be in the best interest of the parties. Too much emphasis on precedence established by adjudication awards may introduce too much rigidity into the adjudication system. On the other hand, if one were to ignore past awards, the stability and proper administration of the collective agreement could be threatened. To disregard the past would mean repeatedly resolving the same issues through adjudication. This could have an adverse effect on the industrial relations climate in the public sector. The interest of the parties would probably be better served by maintaining uniformity and stability in the adjudication process. Consistency in decisions leads toward accumulation of precedents, which can facilitate standardization of labor relations policy. A permanent core of adjudicators can become expert in the problems confronting the public sector.

In the private sector, one of the frequent criticisms [21] of arbitration is that the arbitrators claim more knowledge about the contract than the parties who drafted the document. Undoubtedly, there are arbitrators who like to upstage the parties in the performance of their duties. This danger is always present regardless of whether one is concerned with the private or public sector. The temptation to play God may be greater with a permanent panel of adjudicators appointed by the government than it would be with adjudicators appointed directly by the parties. Should the parties become disenchanted with the publicly supplied adjudicators, they always have a way out. They can decide to utilize the services of private arbitrators.

Whether the Canadian system of grievance adjudication will shift toward publicly supplied or privately selected adjudicators will depend on the nature of adjudication awards, Board policies regarding adjudication costs, and whether or not there is legislative amendment of the statute. In the event that the parties decide to move toward privately selected arbitrators, it is strongly suggested that legislation prevent the emergence of *ad hoc* arbitration in the public sector. The pros and cons of *ad hoc* arbitration are beyond the scope of this paper. However, there is enough literature available on the subject to suggest that *ad hoc* arbitration would not be desirable for the public domain.

## Conclusions

Adjudication is an important tool for resolving disputes that cannot be settled satisfactorily through joint meetings of labor and management representatives at the various levels of the grievance machinery. There is no doubt that in the private sector, many strikes over unresolved grievances are prevented because of the existence of the arbitration process. The usefulness of arbitration is best illustrated by its popularity. Over 90 per cent of contracts in the private sector contain arbitration clauses.

In spite of its significance and its acceptance, arbitration has its hazards. In some instances, the presence of arbitration leads to abdication by the parties of the responsibility to settle their problems without third-party intervention. In some cases in the private sector, when the parties have difficulties resolving their differences at the bargaining table, they may write certain paragraphs of their contracts in general language. This, in turn, opens the agreement to many different interpretations. Although this approach may facilitate the signing of an agreement and prevent a strike, it may also set the stage for future arbitrations. The probability of the parties delegating their bargaining obligations to a third party are greater when the adjudication process is free, fast, and easily available. Frequent use of adjudication could lead to a weakening of the grievance machinery. In many companies in the private sector, unions and management try very hard to resolve their grievances at the lowest possible level of the grievance procedure. They recognize that this not only avoids arbitration, but it also leads to better labor-management relations. This private approach is a good model for the public sector to follow. It is imperative that the public sector grievance machinery not become a referral agency, but rather become a filtering mechanism through which only the most difficult cases move toward adjudication. One way of strengthening grievance machinery and discouraging excessive adjudication would be to report publicly on the percentage of grievances that could have been legally referred to adjudication, but that instead were solved at the various steps of the grievance procedure.

Public criticism of superfluous use of adjudication may be helpful in averting potential abuse of the adjudication process. So far, the number of cases that went to adjudication has been relatively small. However, the Canadian system in its present form has the possibility for too rapid a growth. Such growth would not necessarily be in the best interest of the parties. Measures to prevent such a development should probably be formulated now.

To conclude, the major drawback of adjudication is to have a third party make determinations with which the direct participants have to live. In the final analysis, there is no ideal substitute for the parties settling their dispute by themselves. After all, no outsider knows as much about the circumstances of each case as the parties themselves. The best adjudication procedure is one that is used in moderation. The ideal system should have enough incentive for the parties to direct their utmost efforts toward resolution of their problems without outside intervention.

## REFERENCES

1. The Public Service Staff Relations Act, 1967, Section 2 (P).
2. Public Service Staff Relations Board, *First Annual Report, 1967-1968*, p. 40, Queen's Printer, Ottawa, 1968.
3. The PSSR Board *Regulations and Rules of Procedure*, Part 3, Section 36-57.
4. The PSSR Board, *Regulations and Rules of Procedure*, Section 38 (2).
5. *Regulations and Rules of Procedure*, Section 39 (1).
6. *Regulations and Rules of Procedure*, Section 42.
7. The PSSR Act, Section 92.
8. The PSSR Act, Section 94.
9. The PSSR Act, Section 94, (2) (b).
10. The PSSR Act, Section 94, (2) (a).
11. The PSSR Board, *Fifth Annual Report*, 1971-1972, p. 44, Information Canada, Ottawa, 1972.
12. *Fifth Annual Report*, p. 40.
13. H. W. Arthurs, *Collective Bargaining by Public Employee Unions in Canada: Five Models*, p. 51, p. 160, fn. 95, The University of Michigan—Wayne State University, Ann Arbor, 1971.
14. The PSSR Act, Section 97 (1).
15. The PSSR Board, *Third Annual Report*, 1969-1970, p. 42, Information Canada, Ottawa, 1971.
16. The PSSR Act, Section 21.
17. The PSSR Act, Section 90 (2).
18. Harry Arthurs, "Adjudication" Joint Conference on Collective Bargaining in

Federal Public Service (AFL-CIO, CLC) Niagara Falls, Ontario, Canada, November 20, 1968. An unpublished paper, p. 6.
19. According to Professor H. W. Arthurs, 60 per cent of adjudication cases are disposed of by adjudicators within 60 days, p. 8.
20. H. W. Arthurs, *Collective Bargaining by Public Employee Unions in Canada: Five Models*, p. 51.
21. Carl H. Hageman, The pros and cons of labor arbitration, *Personnel*, 37(3):27-35, May-June, 1960.

*          *          *

Dr. Herman is a professor and head of the economics department at the University of Cincinnati. He has authored numerous books and articles relating to economics and collective bargaining. He has also served as an economist with the Department of Labor in Canada. Professor Herman has been a speaker at conferences and seminars throughout the U.S. and Canada.

## Discussion Questions

1. What does the term "adjudication" mean in relation to U.S. grievance methods?
2. Describe the three specific categories of grievances that may be referred to adjudication under Canadian law, and discuss the value of excluding other issues.
3. The Canadian statute distinguishes between the rights of an individual employee and the rights and interest of all the members of the bargaining unit. Discuss and give examples of when such rights might agree and when they might differ.

*Reprinted from Journal of Collective Negotiations in the Public Sector, Winter, 1974*